Thoughts I Hope You've Had Too

Thoughts I Hope You've Had Too

James Steger

iUniverse, Inc.

New York Lincoln Shanghai

Thoughts I Hope You've Had Too

iUniverse, Inc.

For information address:
iUniverse, Inc.
2021 Pine Lake Road, Suite 100
Lincoln, NE 68512
www.iuniverse.com

ISBN: 0-595-32102-X

Printed in the United States of America

Contents

Introduction

This is not a "feel good" book. Unless reading my thoughts will make you feel good that someone is finally saying what you have been thinking.

What I have written is for anyone who feels frustrated, threatened, or perhaps even overwhelmed by daily life in America today. I hope you will be relieved after reading this to know that you are not the only person who feels that way.

In the past 25 years or so, in less than a person's lifetime, I have seen so many disappointing changes take place in our society that I could remain silent no longer.

I am a product of a "middle class" upbringing. I was not raised with the wealthy, and I was fortunate that we were not poor either. I grew up with a mother and a father, as did most of my friends. Whatever problems existed I had a sense that there were people working on the solutions.

My life seemed normal to me because it was similar to the lives of those with whom I grew up. I realize that there are many people who may have had a different upbringing than I.

Perhaps what I have written will not make sense to them. I am hoping, however, that there will be plenty of others like me whose experiences are similar to mine and who therefore feel the way I do.

It's possible that no one will even care what I think. I did not finish college. I am not an "expert" sought out by others. I am not wealthy or powerful or even influential. I don't have my own television show or newspaper column. I am outnumbered, insignificant and unimportant. I am an easy target for anyone who wants to contest what I am writing.

On the other hand, since I live and work "in the trenches" with so many of you it's possible that I am expressing what you are feeling too.

Everyday I hear more and more people sadly resigning themselves to a reluctant acceptance of the way things are. I see veiled fear in their eyes. I see optimism and hope slowly waning.

I cannot understand why there is no public outcry demanding that we stop the ever-increasing erosion of our society. On the other hand, I realize that in today's hyper-critical climate even the slightest hint of what might be perceived as "criticism" will be met with resistance and some kind of counterattack. It seems no one is ever guilty of anything anymore.

Much of what I am expressing will be subjected to second-guessing, misinterpretation, and perhaps even outrage. I wonder if cries for help and cries for change have been muted by our current tendency to "shoot the messenger."

There are times, however, when someone needs to say something. Somebody needs to step up and say, "Hey, the Emperor isn't wearing any clothes!"

Maybe what I have written is nothing more than the ranting of a middle-aged man. I have thought over and over, "Am I just being my dad?" We all know how the "older" generation historically thinks that the younger generation is contributing to the demise of our country. I am certain there is an element to that in the way I am feeling. However, I am afraid that this feeling may be more accurate now than at any other time in recent history.

I do know this. In past few decades I have seen every code by which so many of us once lived crumble. Search though I may, I can only find fragments of what once were the pillars of our society. If I am wrong, then I am just a worrier, an old guy acting and sounding like an old guy. If I am doing that, dismiss me and continue to dance happily into your future.

On the other hand, if enough people are feeling as I do, perhaps there may still be a way that, together, we can turn this great ship we call "America" and sail in a new direction.

I do realize that there are numerous good things occurring in our country today. I am grateful for all of them. However I am tired of bad things getting hidden or minimized by the expectation that we must mention something good every time a problem is addressed. I am frustrated by our tendency to be "politically correct" thereby coating over things that need to be said.

I know there are many wonderful people—students, parents and families in this country. We have fantastic advantages. Each of us is blessed to be living in America. The list of wonderful people, places and things in this country is indeed lengthy. However, this book was not written about them. This book was written for them.

Perhaps reading my thoughts will inspire those of you who feel as I do to make your feelings known. Let's not "go quietly into that dark night."

What follows are my opinions and observations of the very real situations I feel are threatening all of us today. These are simply my thoughts. They are thoughts I hope you've had too.

We are Our Only Predators

Human beings have been blessed. In our world there are no other creatures who pose a threat to our species. We aren't the biggest, the strongest, the fastest or even the most adaptive. There are countless other creatures that inhabit our world and yet we have taken over the planet-to the detriment of many of them. No other creatures can stop us. We have no natural enemies. We are the top of the food chain. I think this has a definite downside.

We don't have to become smarter, quicker, stronger, or more versatile. We are also not compelled to constantly keep an edge individually. Since we are not threatened by a predatory species (other than each other) we can let down our guard. We can become sloppy. We aren't motivated to come together like other species who seek shelter from their enemies because there is "strength in numbers."

Science fiction writers in the past who were contemplating this reality wrote stories about invaders from space coming to earth. This concept made our weaknesses more apparent.

In that scenario we seemed less intelligent and much more vulnerable. In those stories, all humans rallied together for our mutual survival. Countries which were once longtime enemies became allies.

These storylines gave us a different perspective. They showed us how trivial, inhumane and selfish we are. We learned that the world could indeed live in peace and in a spirit of cooperation-if we were being threatened by an alien attack.

As crazy as this premise may sound, the lesson is unavoidable. We humans have embraced many of our vices because there is no real force stopping us. We simply do not have the discipline needed to create this "perfect" world on our own.

Imagine if humans had to live in fear of some natural enemy. We would not only improve collectively, we would be forced to become better individually.

We would have to be more wary, quicker, sharper, and more cunning. As humans, we would still possess the ability to care for the weak, the sick and elderly. However, the able-bodied would have to sharpen their skills constantly. Those who remained agile and sharp-witted would have a better chance of making it to the elderly stage of life than those who chose to be lazy, out of shape or careless.

Many of our vices would instantly decline. Drug, alcohol and tobacco usage would be minimized. Such behaviors would just be too risky. Overeating? No way. It would be too dangerous.

What about our overall cunning, intelligence, and mutual cooperation? Would they improve if our survival depended upon it?

In nature, it is virtually impossible for an older, weaker, less cunning animal to kill one that is stronger and smarter. Tragically, in our world, nature's rule of "survival of the fittest" does not apply. The weakest, most dim-witted human can easily kill a brighter, stronger human. Indeed, it happens every single day.

Those who are great thinkers, or highly skilled physically, the dreamers, artists, inventors, builders are all equally vulnerable. Not a day goes by that a less productive, weaker person does not snuff out the life of someone who was an asset, or who one day would have been an asset, to our world.

Think about that. In the time it took you to read this section, at least one such life was just extinguished. It will happen again as you read the next section. What will be the final outcome of this reality? Too bad it would take an attack by "martians" to force us to become better humans.

It also seems to me that another result of our superiority over all other living creatures is that we are "evolving" in two directions.

Like other creatures, humans seem to be getting bigger, stronger, and perhaps even more intelligent. We continue to make advances in virtually every aspect of our lives.

We see great thinkers inventing more, developing more, and discovering more. We see athletes able to perform at higher and higher levels. We are healthier. We are also living longer.

However, are we not also facing more and more sicknesses, disorders, syndromes, and the like? On one hand many of the diseases and illnesses that were once considered deadly have either been wiped out, or no longer pose a threat. But have there not been other illnesses, and physical handicaps springing up to replace them?

While other living creatures seem to only make advances in their evolutions, humans seem to make advances, coupled with setbacks. As more and more progress is made in medicine, newer or stronger diseases or physical deformities seem to be keeping pace. As humans grow in height, strength and overall health, as we evolve, why are we still facing so many physical, mental and emotional disorders? Why are we unable to leave such things behind even after centuries of "evolution?"

Many "experts" consider our current society to be the most self-medicating society in history. As we evolve shouldn't the need for medications begin to decrease?

In America, arguably the best country in the world, lifestyles have certainly contributed to many of these problems. While certain challenges being faced in other countries may be the result of a lack of resources or of circumstances beyond their control, we Americans, in many ways, are causing and even embracing our own self-destruction.

As I mentioned earlier, with no natural enemies or other predatory creatures threatening us, it's easy to get complacent. We are free to engage in behaviors which are harmful and which have profoundly negative effects on us. Some of the challenges we are facing are the direct result of these behaviors.

Here is a fact that should be very unsettling. The leading cause of preventable death in America is smoking. In second place and rapidly moving up is obesity and the lack of physical activity. What does that say about America and Americans? The two leading causes of death in this country are the result of behaviors that we are choosing! I believe a case could be made that both causes are the result of an overall lack of discipline.

Consider how these chosen behaviors in our American lifestyle have quietly and relentlessly impacted our society. How many medical challenges are we having to deal with that are the result of drug, alcohol, or tobacco abuse? I am not only referring to the users. I am referring to their offspring as well. What percentage of mental and/or physical disorders, learning disabilities, etc. in children are the results of the use of drugs, alcohol and tobacco products by their parents? What would be the impact on our society if NO ONE engaged in these behaviors? Isn't that an astounding concept? Imagine what that could mean!

I sometimes wonder, at any given moment, on any given day, how many of the people living in America are being harmed by their use of drugs, alcohol and/or tobacco. Right now, right this moment, for example, what percentage of Americans are "under the influence"? What is the overall effect on them individually and on the rest of us collectively? Is there any other species on this planet choosing to self-destruct this way? Is such behavior holding us back or advancing us forward?

If there were predatory animals, other than ourselves, stalking us would our destructive behaviors change in any way? If the answer is "yes" to that question, then the implication is that we could change if we were forced to for our own survival. Isn't it a shame that we don't just choose to become better because our intelligence compelled us to, and our self-discipline made us able to?

Another factor contributing to our overall weakness would have to be our expectation of "instant gratification." Americans today have to be comfortable—instantly and at all times. We no longer have to overcome as many inconveniences or discomforts as those in the past. Even people living today in many other countries have to deal with problems most Americans are no longer facing. I believe this has also contributed to our being "soft."

It wasn't so long ago when Americans had to learn to live with being wet in the rain, cold in the winter and hot in the summer. This was true not only when they were working outside, but also while in their own homes. They had to work harder to get their food and shelter. Everyday life involved more labor and took more time than that to which we have become accustomed. Life in the past did not offer most of the everyday comforts readily available to us, but there were some advantages.

Hunting, planting, harvesting, building, cleaning and traveling each in their own way made a person stronger and kept them better conditioned. When one's lifestyle is physically demanding, self-discipline becomes almost second nature. A tougher lifestyle meant tougher people.

Look at us now. We expect our needs to be met instantly. Flip a switch, there's our light. Set the thermostat, and there's our heat and cooling. Turn on a spigot, there's our water. Take out a meal from the refrigerator, pop it into the microwave and two minutes later, it's ready to eat.

I don't think many of us would want to return to the hardships of the past. Many of us would be ill prepared for survival under such "harsh" conditions. Today, however, we are faced with our own challenges.

Since there is nothing preventing most of us from easily getting the comforts we desire we must learn to exercise the self-restraint needed to keep from over-indulging. As we get more, we must also learn to resist more. Food for example, is so readily available that we must resist the temptation to eat whenever we feel like it—just because we can. Many of us no longer find ourselves having to do intense physical labor. Therefore, we must take it upon ourselves to stay in shape by regularly exercising.

We must seek balance and moderation in all things. If we do not, the comforts we now enjoy will become contributors to our eventual demise. In this day and age there are too many people who lack self-discipline. There are too many people indulging in any number of detrimental behaviors. There are too many people, like it or not, who are contributing to our "backward" evolution.

While millions of Americans are watching their weight, joining gyms, eating healthier, and avoiding harmful substances, millions of others are overeating, avoiding exercise, and/or abusing drugs, alcohol, and/or tobacco. Still others may be doing some combination of each. How much longer can the trends in both directions continue?

When will Americans stop sugar-coating these weaknesses? When will we stop patronizing each other and start to tell it like it is? The truth is that in America, we humans are not only growing stronger we are also getting weaker.

The fact that so many of us are killing ourselves by willingly inhaling the smoke of a burning plant (which we paid to do) is obscene. In addition we are stuffing so much food down our throats that we have become the fattest country in the world. That is not only embarrassing, it is disgusting.

(Here is some sobering information from the Centers for Disease Control, CDC).

The profile of diseases contributing most heavily to death, illness, and disability among Americans changed dramatically during the last century. Today, chronic diseases—such as cardiovascular disease (primarily heart disease and stroke), cancer, and diabetes—are among the most prevalent, costly, and preventable of all health problems. Seven of every 10 Americans who die each year, or more than 1.7 million people, die of a chronic disease.

"Actual" causes of death are defined as lifestyle and behavioral such as smoking and physical inactivity that contribute to this nation's leading killers including heart disease, cancer, and stroke.

In 2000, the most common actual causes of death in the United States were tobacco (435,000), poor diet and physical inactivity (400,000), alcohol consumption (85,000), microbial agents (e.g., influenza and pneumonia, 75,000), toxic agents (e.g., pollutants and asbestos, 55,000), motor vehicle accidents (43,000), firearms (29,000), sexual behavior (20,000) and illicit use of drugs (17,000).

The direct medical cost associated with physical inactivity was nearly $76.6 billion in the year 2000.

Now it's time for each of us to decide to which part of the evolutionary spectrum we belong. Where do you belong? Are you in the group making us stronger? Or are you in the group making us weaker?

Where do We Draw the Line?

In my opinion we have gone overboard in our insistence on being politically correct. For all intents and purposes, in order to avoid offending anyone and everyone we have fostered an environment in which people can rationalize that all weaknesses or shortcoming are acceptable. We all belong just as we are. What is worse is the fact that no one can hold anyone accountable for their shortcomings without fear of some kind of reprisal. Let me explain.

In our schools, for example, a teacher has to be careful when they tell a student that he/she is lazy or not working up to their potential. In doing so, they run the risk of having a parent accuse the teacher of insulting or berating their son or daughter. In the workplace an employer has to be careful when hiring or firing to insure they don't expose themselves to complaints or lawsuits for "wrongfully" terminating someone or for not hiring a "qualified" candidate due to some perceived prejudice. Coaches in youth sports are pressured into playing everyone on the team, regardless of the individual's performance at practice or his/her skill level. Parents stand at the ready to question or second guess every line up or substitution.

I think it's sad and very harmful that we can no longer tell someone who is lazy that he/she is lazy. If someone is spoiled, they should be told. If you are flawed and someone is genuinely trying to help motivate you or is pointing out these flaws in a constructive way, don't act like it is a crime and the person is a criminal. If you are not performing up to expectations on the job, don't blame the other employees or the employer for mentioning it. If you are doing a poor job of parenting, face up to it and start to work on improving.

Even worse are the people who, after receiving some kind of criticism, immediately start pointing out all the other people who they have decided are just as bad or worse than they are. They seem to believe this is somehow relevant or justifies their own poor performance.

Have you been in a position either professionally, or perhaps you were acting in friendship, when you spoke to someone about an area they needed to improve upon? Did they respond by asking you, "Well what about.......are you going to talk to him/her too?" "Why are you telling me this? What about the other people who don't do their jobs? Are you going to say the same thing to them?" "What about the mistakes you have made? Do you think you are better than me?" Or the ever famous, "I thought we were friends."

All of us have weaknesses. Sometimes it takes a person to confront us before we face up to them. What is wrong with a teacher, coach, employer or parent telling us what we need to hear? Most people are not driven to be their very best on their own. Sometimes it takes someone to motivate or irritate us into striving to do better. In these situations consider what is being said. If it makes some sense, use it to your advantage. If it does not have any value to you, let it go.

Is the fact that we no longer encourage this practice a good thing? Are we actually better off when, as a society, we have retreated from facing the truth about ourselves? How are we benefiting by penalizing or admonishing the people in our lives who are trying to make us better?

Here is a question I have been thinking about lately. Would our society today accept the behaviors of the demanding, abrupt, "tell it like it is" leaders, who, by being tough and demanding, achieved great things in the past?

Would Vince Lombardi, Herb Brooks, General Patton, and other such leaders be tolerated today? Could the "Miracle on Ice"—the U.S. winning the gold medal in hockey in the 1980 Olympics under coach Herb Brooks—happen in today's athletic atmosphere, with today's athletes and parents? Would Vince Lombardi be allowed to reign over his players the way he did during his tenure with the Green Bay Packers in the 1960s? Even as tough and as disciplined as today's military is, would General Patton's leadership style be accepted?

I am convinced that a strong argument could be made that accomplishments which were once the result of "hardnosed" leadership are rapidly decreasing. Hardnosed leadership is no longer tolerated. People just quit, complain or sue when faced with a leader who pushes them "too hard".

I have another question. How many people do you know who remember their toughest teacher, coach, drill instructor, boss or even parent(s) with the greatest admiration and respect? You may even feel this way yourself. If being tough on people is so bad, why do so many successful people give credit for their success to the most demanding people who influenced their lives? Please don't think by "demanding" I mean only those who scream and yell. I am referring to leaders who had standards and expectations and required everyone over whom they had influence to meet and live up to them.

One great example of a leader who did not scream and yell, but who was very demanding, is John Wooden, the extraordinary basketball coach from UCLA. Look at the results he achieved in a quiet, "gentle" way. He won 10 national championships. However, he never backed down from his expectations or standards. In that sense he was no less demanding than his more vocal counterparts.

During his career, Coach Wooden dealt with one of the most "rebellious" athletes of his day, Bill Walton. Mr. Walton was a "free spirit" caught up in the political and social chaos of the 60s while playing for Coach Wooden at UCLA. Much of what Walton believed was in direct conflict with what Coach Wooden was demanding. I am sure they butted heads numerous times. However, by his own admission, Mr. Walton considers Coach Wooden to be the single most influential person in his life and the primary reason for his success in college, the NBA and in broadcasting.

This is just one example of what "demanding" leadership can produce. There are also numerous other leaders, all with similar standards and expectations, but with differing styles, who were also instrumental in the lives of many successful people. Is it safe to say that in today's childish, it's all about me, "you can't make me" society that even Coach Wooden would not be tolerated?

The bottom line when it came to many of the great teachers, coaches, parents, and other motivators of the past was their uncompromising pursuit of excellence. They were allowed to operate without constant second-guessing or challenges from those over whom they had influence. What does it tell us that under so many of these great leaders that excellence in their "pupils" was actually achieved? Can uncompromising leadership actually be a good thing?

Is there any question that many of the most successful and influential teachers, coaches, and leaders of the past would never be tolerated today by young people and/or their parents (and their lawyers)? How will greatness be achieved now? Who will tomorrow's successful people point to as the reason(s) for their success? And finally, will the level of overall success and achievement in this country be forever compromised because we no longer accept someone else pointing out our weaknesses in an attempt to make us better?

Acceptance of Everyone and Everything

This will be like walking through a minefield. One misstep and I will be caught in a blast of criticism and accusations from the people I was describing previously. These are the folks who sit and wait for even the slightest hint of criticism so they can retaliate with attacks in the media and in the courts. Hopefully what I am trying to say will make sense. This is just basic objectivity, not personal opinion, political leaning or self-righteous judgment. Let's see what the acceptance of this thinking has actually produced and will continue to produce.

When a society accepts, or is forced to accept, every person, every group, and every philosophy, the implication is that there are no harmful or detrimental people, groups, philosophies that could eventually lead to the destruction of the very society that accepted them. In a perfect world there would be no need to differentiate between all the "groups" or philosophies. For in this world everyone would be dedicated to the well-being of everyone else. However, this is not a perfect world. What makes all of this even more complicated is that this country was founded on the principles of freedom and the "pursuit of happiness", not just for a few, but for all men/women.

We have always had some struggle making that a reality. Discrimination and racism have been a constant threat to the philosophy this country was built upon. Perhaps we as humans will always be guilty to varying degrees of such behavior. However, it seems that in our effort to eliminate all discrimination we have retreated from the possibility that maybe presently there are people or groups who need to be excluded.

I realize how this sounds. I know the standard responses to this will be, "Who do you suggest we exclude?" "Who is going to determine who stays and who leaves?" "What makes one group better than another?" "If you exclude one individual or group then who will be next?"

Who today wants to face the wrath of any group, regardless of how small, by pointing out the harm that group may cause, or is causing, to all the other members of society? Who wants to face the hassle and expense of an almost certain law suit filed by an attorney claiming he/she is protecting the group's or individual's civil rights?

Is it possible, however, at some point that our willing or forced acceptance of every individual and every group will eventually lead to our own downfall? Can a free society protect itself from that which can cause its own demise? Are there any natural "filters" that will prevent harmful influences from thriving in such a society?

It's time for a reality check. Even though America represents one of the greatest democracies in history, it is simply not possible to accommodate every single belief, philosophy and lifestyle that comes along. In order for a democracy to be successful people have to be willing to compromise certain individual expectations for the good of the whole. No matter how you cut it, if no individual or groups are willing to make certain sacrifices then the net result is a fractured society which is constantly in conflict.

A society is nothing more than a very large family. How successful would any family be, regardless of how small, if no one in that family was willing to compromise? The reality is each member can't do everything that they want, when they want, every time they want. It is essential that there is some give and take. Sometimes it's possible to accommodate the needs of one member; however, more often an individual's needs may be outweighed by those of the other members. Isn't that the basic foundation of a democracy—majority rules? If individual demands could destroy a small family, what would such demands do to an entire society?

Group dynamics are group dynamics. The same principles apply to any group. They cannot be ignored if collective harmony is desired. Can a company be successful if every person in the company does whatever they feel they deserve to be doing? Can a team be successful if each player demands that the coach do what each one wants? Even animals that live in herds or packs understand this. When it's time to move or hunt they don't all stand around trying to make sure they take into account the wants and desires of each member of the herd. Those that refuse to do what the herd is doing are left behind.

We are faced with a tough moral question. Will we simply "live and let live" regardless of the consequences or will we begin to stand up to groups or individuals who pose a threat to the majority? Will individuals or outnumbered groups be willing to sacrifice or compromise their demands if it would ultimately benefit the well-being of the majority?

This may be a tough pill to swallow—but is there any other way? Such questions and considerations have become necessary at this time in our history—when they were not in the past—because we are faced with so many conflicting attitudes and demands. Never before have so many demanded so much with so few willing to accept anything less.

I know there are groups and organizations that will claim if we take away the rights of any individual than everyone else's rights will be threatened. Really? I say it is possible to have guidelines which are fair and logical, which won't start us down the proverbial "slippery slope" we are constantly warned about.

Whether it is nationally or locally, these guidelines should reflect the expectations of the majority. This would establish a basic set of standards and laws by which everyone would be expected to live—even if it meant some compromising by individuals or small groups. I think it is safe to say that our forefathers never envisioned the abuse of majority rights and freedoms that would occur at the hands of individuals taking advantage of the Constitution/Bill of Rights. The insanity we live with today could not have been foreseen some 200 years ago.

Our forefathers certainly envisioned a society in which the majority would determine who the leaders would be and by what laws citizens would live. Is that true today? Is the majority making the decisions today? Have we not gone overboard in protecting an individual's rights to such a degree that the majority no longer has a voice? Have we been so busy protecting the "rights" of each and every person or group that we inadvertently ignored the wants and needs of the majority? Why should one individual or even a small group have the right to do away with something that the majority of the country may want? It is shocking to me how many people there are today who have absolutely no regard for anyone but themselves. Such people complain and demand constantly until they get what they want.

Here's an example of what I mean. Let's say there is a large group of people at a party all dancing to country music. In walks a person who doesn't particularly enjoy country music. In the past, that person out of respect and courtesy for everyone else would tolerate the music and proceed to enjoy the friendship and activities. Today, there are far too many people who, after listening to the music, would demand that rock music, for example, also be played. If the majority ignored this demand and continued playing country the individual might sit and pout or act in some other equally inappropriate way.

To take this example a step farther, there are many people today who would be so determined to get rock played that after arguing with the group and disrupting the party they would then go and get a lawyer. Together they would stand before a judge demanding that rock music be played not just at that party but all future parties as well.

Why is it that in today's society even the smallest group or one individual feels that it's their right to get what they want irrespective of what the majority may want? People today are actually proud when they contest an accepted tradition, philosophy or law. It's a shame more people don't take into account how everyone else may feel. There are far too many "whiners" today. One person can make the rest of us adjust to whatever the courts determine is his/her individual right. Shouldn't that be the other way around?

If an individual or group decides one day, for example, that the American flag should be changed because it symbolizes a country that represents capitalism and as such is in direct conflict with their beliefs will the courts then rule that our flag will need to be revised?

If an individual claims that they are being unfairly treated by the playing of the National Anthem before a sporting event will that have to stop too?

If an individual claims that any and all references to God are offensive will we have to revise everything containing such references?

Whenever the courts rule in favor of one individual, against the wishes of the majority, thereby forcing everyone else to comply with the wishes of the individual, isn't that pretty much the same as a monarchy?

Silly you say? Haven't the trends we have all lived through recently been doing exactly that?

America is a democracy and like it or not a modern democracy cannot accommodate everyone. There are simply too many people clamoring to get what they want. Attempting to please everyone will have the same effect on our society that doing so would have on a family, a team, a company, an army, or even a herd. The final result will be chaos. The time has come to remember the foundation of a true democracy—majority rules. Collective harmony must take precedence over individual satisfaction. When in doubt go with the majority.

The "Separation of Church and State"

The First Amendment of our Constitution, as it pertains to religion reads: "*Congress shall make no law respecting an establishment of religion or prohibiting the free exercise thereof....*" It is astounding to me how misunderstood this very simple concept has become.

This amendment, in part, is the foundation for religious freedom in America. However, thanks to continued misinterpretation and misrepresentation it has been turned upside down from its original intention and concept.

The First Amendment and its supposed establishment of "separation of church and state" is often used to justify the removal of religious references, practices and symbols from anything having to do with government. The original intention of this amendment was the exact opposite. Here are the facts.

The first amendment of the Constitution was written by our forefathers as a way to prevent Congress (the government) from interfering with the establishment of religion or "prohibiting the free exercise thereof." This was one of the primary reasons the creators of the Constitution/Bill of Rights came to America in the first place. The last thing any of them was concerned about, or trying to prevent, was the interference of religion in government matters.

Even more misunderstood is the fact that nowhere in the Constitution/Bill of Rights is there any mention of "separation of church and state". Whenever someone refers to such concept as though it were included in the Constitution they are mistaken. The "separation" of church and state was actually first mentioned in a letter written by

Thomas Jefferson to the Danbury Baptists eleven years after the Constitution had been ratified.

In this letter, Jefferson was stating his support of "this separation" because of its protection of the free practice of religion, not for its protection of government *from* religion. How did we get to the point we are at now?

If people feel that there is too much religion or religious influence in government and want to take steps to "correct" this, fine. But please don't allow them to use the Constitution, the Bill of Rights or the words, "separation of church and state" to justify their actions.

This nation was founded by people who believed in and prayed to "God". Their beliefs were so strong they purposely included references to and images of God in virtually every aspect of government. Here are just a few examples of government throughout history continuing to include God in government:

First, in the Declaration of Independence our forefathers wrote, "...all men are *created* equal, that they are endowed by their *Creator* with certain inalienable rights..."

They didn't write, "All men have evolved equally." They didn't say, "All men are born equal." Nor did they write, "All men have the right to be equal." In addition, their reference to, "...their Creator..." is indicative of their belief in God whose power they were acknowledging.

There is no question of their intention to include God in the government they were establishing. So much so the name of God is mentioned at the beginning of the very declaration by which they were announcing their independence.

Lesser known are words in a cover letter which was attached to the Declaration of Independence itself when it was first sent to the British Authorities. In the letter, written by John Hancock, is yet another respectful reference to God:

> *"Gentlemen, Altho it is not possible to forsee the consequences of human actions, yet it is nevertheless a duty we owe ourselves and*

posterity in all our public councils to decide in the best manner we are able and to trust the event to That Being who governs both causes and events, so as to bring about his own determinations."

In this paragraph John Hancock is acknowledging not only God Himself, but his own belief that God "...governs both causes and events, so as to bring about his own determinations." It's easy to see that it was second nature for the founding fathers to think in terms of God at such a critical time. Indeed they were hoping this very risky endeavor of theirs would be pleasing to God and thereby blessed by Him.

Next, the words, "...so help you God." which are spoken by every person about to testify in a court of law were thought to have borrowed from the English court of law. The founders of this country believed so strongly in God and in His power they included that phrase when a person was "swearing" to tell the truth.

Belief in, and fear of, a just God was so accepted that it was felt by making the reference to Him would compel the person taking the oath to be truthful—lest they answer to God. They did not choose phrases like, "...so help you King George." or "...because I know if I lie I will get into a lot of trouble with my new government."

This respect and willingness to acknowledge God in the U.S. government was evident once again in 1865 when an act of Congress mandated the addition of the words, "In God We Trust" on all gold and silver coins. The phrase was later added on other coins as well.

In 1954 another act of Congress added the words, "...under God..." in the Pledge of Allegiance. Two years later, July 30th, 1956 a law passed in the 84th Congress and was signed by then President Eisenhower which made the words, "In God We Trust" the national motto of the United States.

Since then every person living in America is living in a country whose national motto is, "In God We Trust." That's right, every single American citizen living in this country for the past nearly fifty years has been living in a country whose national motto is, "In God We Trust."

It is quite clear throughout the history of our country, beginning with the founding fathers and continuing through 1956, some 180 years in all, that the government of these United States has had an allegiance to God. All of the subsequent references to God and the laws mandating them were written and approved by lawmakers who were merely continuing the beliefs and intentions of each of the previous generations of lawmakers who had come before them.

This country and everything about it was originally established by and for "God-fearing" people. For decades this was understood by those who came here and by those who were born here. It seems that many people have forgotten that.

Even worse, there are people today who are acting like righteous avengers as they continuously challenge or criticize the very foundations, philosophies and beliefs upon which this country was built. Too many of us have stood silently in the shadows of this once better land, while ill-informed "citizens", with the support of misguided lawyers make constant attempts to chip away at what were once regarded as sacred truths.

Why have we gone out of our way to exclude God from our government? If we use the Constitution as the guide by which we settle questions of freedoms and rights, why have we been ignoring the obvious intentions of those who created the constitution in the first place? And why now? Are we the first generation to truly grasp the meaning of the First Amendment?

Are Americans today so arrogant that we feel we understand the constitution and how to interpret it better than any generation that came before us? Are we somehow now more enlightened than those who penned our Constitution and all the generations that followed—until now?

Whether you like it or not, God has been an integral part of the American government since this country was founded. Stop listening to people who are claiming otherwise. Stop listening to people demanding to change that. There are plenty of countries in the world which don't include God in their government. This is not one of them.

I would like to submit to you that we acknowledge the words, "Congress will make no laws respecting the establishment of religion or prohibiting the free exercise there of…" actually mean that our elected government officials will not and can not stop anyone from establishing a religion or exercising the free expression of their chosen religion.

I believe the original concept of "separation of church and state" meant that government could not interfere with religion. It was not intended to be the excuse people could use to remove religion from government. I also maintain that for anyone who is not religious, the freedom provided to them in the First Amendment protects them from being forced to practice any and all religions.

People don't have to believe in God. However, it does not give those groups or individuals the right to prevent everyone else from exercising their belief in God whenever and wherever they choose—including in our schools and in our government.

It really doesn't matter how many people try to convince you otherwise. History has shown that in America it is not in government, but "In God We Trust."

Institutional Erosion

Am I the only one to have noticed that most Americans have lost respect for virtually every group or institution we once considered as models in our society? Those we would point to as positive examples for ourselves and our children, are now corrupt or at the very least, trying to overcome some kind of controversy.

Consider the recent scandals associated with the Presidency of the United States, all levels of government, law enforcement, organized religion, the military and military institutions, education/educators, medicine, sports/athletes and all sizes of businesses. It seems that scandal and corruption abound. Are there any "institutions" which have not succumbed to some kind of corruption or scandal?

What is equally disconcerting to me is that we are so overcome by the sheer magnitude of the scandal and controversy in our daily lives that we tend to overlook them while "lashing out" against "targets" which are smaller and easier to hit By that I mean we will rise up in anger and dismay over a single incident or against a single person instead of against larger more deserving offenders like government, politicians, corporations, associations, etc.

For example, some of our most impassioned reactions to "scandals" recently have been directed against two individuals. One was Janet Jackson whose now infamous "wardrobe malfunction" nearly brought all life as we know it to a grinding halt. The other was Steve Irwin's (The Crocodile Hunter) incident of feeding a crocodile while holding his infant son in one arm. Again, the world rose up like a self-righteous warrior dedicated to seeing this man pay for his dastardly doings.

Regardless of what you think of these two situations, they pale in comparison to the destructive evil that exists in our society—and in the world. The outrage that erupted over these two incidents would lead one to believe that seeing criminals kidnap, rape and murder our children on a regular basis would send us into a frenzied whirlwind of humanity demanding justice!

Shouldn't the villagers be storming the castle, torches in hand, demanding that their leaders put an end to these crimes? Why did we spend so much energy objecting to Janet Jackson and Steve Irwin when true corruption is at our very doorstep? Do we not see or do we not care that evil roams freely in our schools, it is lurking in our churches, it resides in our government and rules our boardrooms?

Generally speaking, I suppose there have always been scandals or corruption in all institutions—even the ones we once revered. It also seems that these controversies are not only more numerous, but they are also more serious, and growing ever more corrupt. We now know that corruption, greed, and dishonesty are woven into the very fabric of our society. Perhaps it has always been that way. Perhaps it will always be.

Why can't we seem to mount any serious threat to the groups, companies, and institutions corrupting our society? I think most Americans are cynical and distrusting of all of them. Yet in most cases feel powerless to do anything to change things. Is it now our destiny to live this way?

We stand at the ready to swarm down upon the next easy target which is "guilty" of offending our sensibilities. All the while passively accepting the manipulation and deception heaped upon us by our once revered institutions.

The "Institution of Marriage"

What about the "institution of marriage"? This institution has been slowly eroding over the past few decades. The divorce rate is now at 50% nationally. It is even higher in some states. Do you ever find yourself, while attending a wedding thinking, "I wonder how long it will be until they get divorced"? It's sad that staying married has become so difficult. It's too bad more couples have not been able do what it takes to insure the success of their marriages.

It seems to me that our parents and/or grandparents lived in a society in which divorce was considered to be immoral or at the very least, unacceptable. "Back in the day" husbands and wives who were not happy in their marriages would still stay together "for the sake of the children." They would find the means to keep the family together. Many did so without complaining or acting like martyrs.

The people with whom I grew up had parents and grandparents who stayed married. The same was true in my family. We were exposed to arguments between parents or to parents who didn't show affection towards each other. There were children who undoubtedly realized that their parents were not happy in the marriages. We experienced many different kinds of marriages, but very few of us ever experienced any kind of a divorce.

The bottom line was that husbands and wives stayed together in spite of whatever problems they may have encountered because they felt it was the right thing to do. This practice helped to produce children who went on to become the "greatest generation" written about by NBC anchor Tom Brokaw. Consider the achievements of the "greatest generation" in technology, medicine, and space exploration, etc. It would be difficult to argue against Mr. Brokaw's assertion.

Then along came the experts who argued that staying in a marriage in which one or both partners is unhappy isn't healthy for anyone in the family—including the children. The divorce rate began to climb, slowly at first but then eventually reaching the 50% rate of today. Families started to break up. Children had to adjust to different combinations of parents. Now here we are.

How do you think we're doing today? Is our society better off now that we are free to dissolve our marriages when they become inconvenient? Since unhappy parents have been encouraged to separate are the children really benefiting more? Do you sometimes wonder if having parents stay in a marriage, even an unhappy one, was as detrimental as we were being told? I do.

Even though divorce is an accepted practice today, each breakup does have an effect on the children. Like it or not, it splinters, even fractures, the emotional security they once experienced. It creates trauma and does have short and long term effects on the children caught in the middle. Perhaps parents aren't even aware of the damage being done to their children. They might be in denial or perhaps the children aren't showing their true emotions.

I am not referring to the breakup of marriages in which one of the parents is abusing the other, and/or the children. I am speaking only of marriages that break up simply because they break down. One partner becomes bored or he/she finds someone else. Perhaps only one partner is making an effort or one or both partners are just plain selfish.

What would the net result in our society be if husbands and wives "sucked it up" and dedicated their lives to the happiness and well-being of their children instead of themselves?

What would it be like if each partner put the other's happiness above their own? These are choices, nothing more. Every day we make a choice as to whom we are going to make happy and satisfy that day. Too often we are choosing ourselves.

Keeping a marriage together is difficult. It's damn difficult. Sacrifices have to be made almost daily. There may be periods when the husband or wife—or both—are convinced the love they once had is gone. Too bad.

It doesn't matter if the "grass is greener" somewhere else. (And we all know that is seldom the case anyway). If you have children then you have a responsibility to put them first. Not just one of the parents. Both parents have to commit. Find joy in parenting together. Be partners in providing happiness to your children. Give when you need to give. Take less.

Watching your children dance and laugh and sing and run is a joy-even if you are doing it with the spouse you feel you no longer love. Besides, it's at times like these, seeing your children laughing in all their innocence, you might even feel proud of both of your efforts.

Marriage provides the most basic foundation from which families grow. Marriage teaches teamwork, sacrifice, commitment, loyalty and love.

Divorce teaches children that nothing is forever. It makes them feel that they can't trust anyone. If you can't trust your mommy and daddy who does that leave? Divorce also bonds children to each other to the exclusion of adults. It causes them to include each other more and include adults less. Consequently they seek acceptance and approval more from their peers. It's almost as if they are raising each other.

Once a child feels betrayed by the parents or gives up because of the pain of losing the security once enjoyed at home, they will fall prey to the first group that accepts them. That is why parents and teachers might see one or more of the children from a family going through a divorce begin to change and it's rarely for the better. It doesn't stop there. What decisions will these children make when they encounter problems in their marriages?

Why are we not more willing to do whatever it takes to keep our families together? Why can't parents compromise in a mature, loving way, so harmony could exist in the family? Not only has divorce become an accepted "solution" for a "troubled" marriage, it is being chosen for less and less "legitimate" reasons.

Is every divorce traumatic to every child? Probably not, but is divorce doing more harm than is being addressed today? Take a good, honest look at today's children. In case you are still unsure, you may be interested in speaking to any teacher who has been teaching for the past several years. Or better yet, talk to a substitute teacher!

Is the prevalence of divorce today in any way a contributing factor to the increase in the issues being faced by our children? Why has there been an increase in teenage suicides, eating disorders, self-mutilation, abusive relationships and other destructive behaviors as the divorce rate increased? I suppose it could be just a coincidence. Is there any evidence that the breakdown in the family structure has <u>not</u> contributed to such behaviors?

People can claim all day long that any number of alternative family arrangements can produce healthy, happy children. I'm sure some have. However, one glance at the dramatic increase in the self-destructive behaviors in our children should tell us that something is wrong somewhere.

Why did the occurrence of so many emotional and mental disorders increase in our children at the same time the basic family structure was disintegrating?

Point fingers where you may but there is no way around the importance of having a mother and a father who love their children. Okay, we tried alternatives. We experimented with variations. They didn't work. It's a simple as that.

Recently even the definition of the word, "marriage" is being challenged. I suppose it was just a matter of time. The definition of "family" has been modified time and time again as more and more variations to the family structure have been introduced and accepted. Working backward from changes in the definition of "family" we have now arrived at the point of examining what should be considered a "marriage".

Regardless of your personal view of this question I think the majority of us would agree that everyone deserves to have equal civil rights. I am more intrigued by the fact that the definition of "marriage" is being challenged at all.

The word, "marriage" has meant basically the same thing for thousands of years. It was considered, more or less, a sacred union between a man and a woman—for life. First the acceptance of divorce began to whittle away at the "for life" part. Now the next "logical" step is to question the "between a man and a woman" part.

Is this a progressive step that humans have finally reached? Does this mean that our society, by examining this once unquestioned "institution", has arrived at an elevated point of enlightenment never before attained by any previous generation in the history of mankind? Or, is the "tinkering" with what a marriage is or is not another indication that we have lost sight of what were once unchallenged foundations of human values and accepted beliefs?

Should deviating from something as fundamental as what a marriage is be encouraged or discouraged? Can those challenging its meaning in any way acknowledge that perhaps marriage is best defined as "a union between a man and a woman" and thereby leave it alone?

Will this "institution" and what is has meant for generations now come under fire, regardless of the consequences, so those who may not meet the longstanding criteria will no longer be left out?

Practical Parenting:

I often wonder if the art and skill of parenting is so complicated in today's world that becoming good parents is virtually unattainable. Let me explain.

In the not so distant past children were all raised pretty much the same way. For one thing, there were not as many choices or lifestyles. Families stayed together. There was a mother and a father and any number of children. Most families were members of a church and to varying degrees participated in some manner in the activities of their church. It was rare for a family to have no religious affiliation of any kind.

Schools were quick to enforce discipline for even the smallest indiscretion. The world for all intents and purposes was the city in which one lived and then more specifically the neighborhood. Parents interacted more with each other and backed up teachers, coaches and police officers. It seemed all adults were watching out for all children. At least that is what I experienced while growing up.

As a child, if I had been involved in some inappropriate behavior which was seen by any adult, I had to be prepared for a scolding from that adult. This was followed by an additional punishment from my own parents after being told about my indiscretion. Adults seemed to relish telling each other about something that either I or one of my friends had done. It seemed that virtually all adults held similar beliefs and principles. They supported each other's efforts.

It made little difference whether I was facing my parents, my friends' parents, my teachers, my coaches, a priest, a minister, a rabbi, a police officer or any other adult. I was treated the same by each. This was a time when adults all had the same values. When growing up, my friends and I realized that the adults had all the power. We were a little respectful, and very fearful of them. It was just better not to cross them.

Of course there were times when we might get into some mischief, but we never considered doing anything defiant or disrespectful, much less violent, when confronted by an adult. It just wasn't worth it.

In addition, it would be shocking, and I do mean, shocking for a young person to "sass" any adult. Silence or responses like, "Yes, ma'am" or "Yes sir" were the norm. We were fully aware of the mysterious bond that linked adults together like some kind of secret army. The smartest thing to do was to just avoid having to face them. So we conducted ourselves accordingly—most of the time.

That has all changed. In my opinion the most damaging change that has occurred in our society in my lifetime is that the structure and organization that once existed between adults has eroded into bits and pieces. Fragments of order and cooperation are all that remains. In short, adults have turned against each other. Adults question other adults and even routinely challenge each other's authority. Challenges by parents made toward (or against) teachers, police officers, coaches, bosses, etc. are commonplace. The structure once provided by adults to the world of children is in ruins.

Today if a child gets in trouble there is a greater chance that the parent will either minimize the situation or worse—they will find someone or something else to blame. Ask any veteran teacher if parents and students accept individual responsibility for their actions the way they once did. Don't we all know parents today whose children can do no wrong?

Today there is little chance that one adult will tell another adult something "bad" about one of their children. There is too much risk today associated with criticizing someone else's child/children. Whether in the form of a lawsuit, or perhaps a verbal or physical confrontation, today's adults know of the potential consequences for "getting involved."

There are plenty of adults today who will look the other way when someone else's children are misbehaving. They do this because there are plenty of parents who will react rudely or violently at the mere mention of something "negative" about their children. These are the parents who are reluctant to discipline their own children. Even worse, they will not permit anyone else to discipline them either. How ridiculous, yet I believe this trend is one of the primary reasons there are now so many unruly, disrespectful and undisciplined children.

Because the "traditional" family structure has eroded and there has been a deterioration of the relationships which once flourished between adults in general, children today are surrounded by chaos and confusion. There seems to be as many ways to raise a child as there are children.

In this disarray parents no longer share the same compass by which they once navigated the waters of child rearing. Add to this the numerous variations of the once traditional family structure and the fact that daily life in general is even more complex and uncertain and you get a recipe for disaster. While parents are battling away at each other the potential influence they can have on their children is being shattered. Other "forces" are moving in and are all competing to claim the children who were left unprotected.

Consider this. In today's world, most parents do not understand or are even aware of what their children have learned, or are learning, from each other. Many parents are also unaware of what their children are being exposed to on the internet, on television, in music and in movies. Today the people with the structured society are the children. When compared to the organized and sophisticated world of children, today's bickering adults don't stand a chance.

One simple example of this is most adults cannot fully use their cell phones or computers. Any teenager or even preteens can make their phones or any piece of modern technology sing and dance. How many adults today can "text message" using all of the codes and symbols and do so with one hand—while not looking! This is just one example.

Most adults are busier than ever earning a living. When combined with the breakdown in the overall family structure, children today spend much more time with each other, either in person, on the computer or on cell phones than they spend with their parents.

In the past, the younger generation may have had some words not used or understood by adults like, "groovy" or "far out". Today the street language used by the younger generation makes them almost bilingual! Today's children have developed a culture just as sophisticated as any we adults may have. Children have become more "independent" and less fearful.

Seriously, in today's society are the children fearful of adults or are adults more fearful of children? There are parents today who are even intimidated by their own children. It is the adult today who tries to avoid the child.

Adults in a mall, for example, try to stay to themselves and avoid the groups of "children" moving about freely with no regard for anyone else. Would any grownup today be surprised, much less shocked, to hear a teen or preteen "mouthing off" to an adult? Haven't we all experienced that? Most adults want to avoid the potential for confrontation with an obnoxious child or a potentially violent loud-mouthed teen so they just walk the other way.

What's worse is that kids today know this. They take advantage of this new hierarchy and nothing is stopping them. Ask any police officer how they are treated by today's youth. Kids today are not at all intimidated by any symbol of authority. They have learned—or should I say—we have taught them, they don't have to be. Whether in school, at home or in court there are few serious consequences anymore for their inappropriate or illegal actions.

In addition, many children today are self-proclaimed lawyers. "I have the right to…." "You're not the boss of me….." "You can't make me…." Unfortunately this detrimental and destructive way of thinking is supported by more and more parents who are unwittingly contributing to their own demise. These parents are actually proud when their children act this way.

Today, there is an ever increasing number of parents and children who immediately want to sue anyone and everyone with whom they have a disagreement. Parents sue other parents. Parents sue schools. Parents sue police. Following their lead, children are now suing their parents.

In general, people today are suing their doctors, their ministers, their neighbors, teachers, coaches, small companies, big companies and on it goes. In short, any time a person doesn't like someone or something or is inconvenienced in some way, there is a very good chance their response will be to file a lawsuit. As we all know there is certainly no shortage of lawyers standing by to assist in this process. That is so disturbing.

The result has been a total breakdown in the boundaries that once existed which prevented or helped to prevent negative behaviors in our children. Not only is discipline lacking in their world, look at the other daily influences that surround them. Profanity, nudity, violence, recklessness, casual sex, drug usage, and any other type of once unacceptable behavior can be seen or heard at any and all times on television, radio, movies, at school and even at home. What has all of this created? Look at the number of crimes, violent and not so violent being committed by younger and younger children.

Here's a statistic for you. Recently, the Department of Justice announced that in 2002 there were 1.5 million children under 18 who had been arrested! Of these, 375,000 were arrested for violent crimes. Imagine, in one year, 375,000 children were arrested for committing violent crimes. The other 1,125,000 were arrested for nonviolent crimes, but had to be arrested nonetheless. That means that over <u>one million</u> children did something that resulted in their being arrested in 2002.

This does not include the number of incidents police were called to deal with which did not result in an arrest. Let me tell you, for a juvenile to actually get arrested today takes some doing. Imagine what the total number of incidents would be if we added in all the occurrences that were handled by teachers, security and police officers that did not result in an arrest.

Today there are murders being committed on a somewhat regular basis by children who have not even reached their teens! What about "drivebys"? How many times in your city do you have one? Are middle school aged children using drugs, having sex, cheating on tests, drinking, sneaking out of the houses, using profanity, joining gangs, defying authority, lying, etc.? In case you don't know, the answer is "yes" to all of those questions. Are the behaviors of our children a reflection of or a reaction to the kind of parents we have been?

Look at the ever-growing number of children with mental and emotional disorders. If our children are as happy and as well adjusted as any previous generation, if we are doing such a good job of parenting, why is the number of teenage suicides steadily growing? Here is another tragic truth:

> *"Teen suicide is becoming more common every year in the United States. In fact, only car accidents and homicides (murders) kill more people between the ages of 15 and 24, making suicide the third leading cause of death in teens and overall in youths ages 10 to 19 years old."*

> —(TeenHealth.com)

> *"In the past 25 years, while the general incidence of suicide has decreased, the rate for those between 15 and 24 has tripled. It is generally considered to be the second or third most common cause of death among adolescents, even though it is seriously underreported".*

> —(Richard O'Connor, PhD, "Teen Suicide")

<u>In the US, the Centers for Disease Control reports that:</u>

- More people die from suicide than from homicide. In 1997, there were 1.5 times as many suicides as homicides.

- Overall, suicide is the eighth leading cause of death for all Americans, and is the <u>third leading cause of death for young people aged 15-24</u>.

<u>The World Health Organization reports:</u>

- In the last 45 years suicide rates have increased by 60% worldwide. Suicide is now among the three leading causes of death among those aged 15-44 (both sexes). Suicide attempts are up to 20 times more frequent than completed suicides.

What about the relatively new phenomenon of teens "cutting" themselves also known as "self-mutilation? This behavior includes, cutting, burning, poking with needles, and picking at one's self.

"Self-mutilation has become a major public health concern as its incidence appears to have risen since the early 1990s. One source estimates that 0.75% of the general American population practices self-mutilation. The incidence of self-mutilation is highest among teenage females, patients diagnosed with borderline personality disorder, and patients diagnosed with one of the dissociative disorders. Over half of self-mutilators were sexually abused as children, and many also suffer from eating disorders"
—(Rebecca J. Frey PhD, "Self-mutilation", Medical Network Inc)

"An estimated 2 million Americans purposely cut or burn themselves. 90% of self-injurers begin cutting as teenagers. The average self-injurer starts at age 14 and continues with increasing severity into their late 20's.

—(deb.arneson.net)

Is it possible that children may have been better off in the past? My own experience of growing up coupled with my experience of raising five children makes me believe that we need to use what once worked as a template for the present and future.

Adults need to support each other the way they once did in the past. The bickering and challenges between adults has to end! Enough is enough.

Parents also need to try harder. It's as simple as that. We need to take parenting more seriously. Today's children are the "products" of today's parents. Even a moderately objective assessment of today's parenting would conclude there is plenty to improve upon.

Children seem to have a better chance of being happy and successful if they have a loving, stable home life. There is nothing new there. But what does that actually mean? To me, it means a mother and a father who stay together. It means discipline, consistently and fairly enforced from an early age. It means all adults in a child's life would preach the same message to that child. The child in turn would be expected to live up to the standards explained to him/her. It means balance.

On a personal note, I was a very strict father, but I also played, danced, wrestled, sang, laughed and shared affection with my children. I ran around the house chasing them acting like a monster. We laughed and occasionally knocked things over causing my wife to yell at all of us. The most important thing was that our kids felt loved. They knew the rules from the time they could understand them.

As parents, my wife and I never deviated from any rule or consequence. We were a team. If I was angry and scolded or spanked (yes I spanked our children) she would be the "comforter". If she was the angry one, then I would be the comforter. Both parents have to support and complement each other. It is critical that your children learn that you mean what you say.

For example, I once told our oldest son when he was about 6 or 7 that if he didn't keep his room clean I would take his bed into our garage where, "....you will have to sleep with the spiders and cockroaches that live in our garage." Well, the next day his room was a mess. Even though I had just returned home from work, and all I wanted to do was relax, I went to his room and started to dismantle his bed. He was crying and begging me not to move it into the garage. I didn't rant or rave. I simply said, "I told you that I was going to move your bed if your room was messy. Your room is messy so you must want me to move your bed in the garage. Okay, I just want you to be happy."

I dragged both mattresses, the frame and all the bedding into the garage. My son was pleading with me the entire time. It broke my heart, but I did not waiver. Naturally, this was one of the times my wife and I teamed up. She "convinced" me to give him another chance. I "resisted" for several minutes and then finally carried everything back into my son's room. I am sure you can guess what I am about to say next. That was the last time we ever had to worry about our son's room being a mess.

Perhaps there are people who would consider this inappropriate parenting. Too bad. The results speak for themselves. It's all about learning that when you choose a behavior you also choose its consequence. Once your children learn that, you are pretty much home free. You will then be free to worry about all the other people in the world who are actually doing something harmful to your children.

Here is another example. When our oldest two daughters were about 6 and 4 I told them not to leave their clothes on the bedroom floor or "I will hang everything I find on your floor on the tree outside so everyone will see how messy you are." I don't know where I came up with that one, but I said it so I knew I would have to stick to it.

I came home from work soon afterward and there were clothes on the floor. I picked up each and every item and proceeded to ceremoniously hang each piece on a separate branch of the tree in our front yard.

It only took seconds for our crying daughters to promise they would never leave clothes on the floor again. Again my wife negotiated a successful settlement. Soon all of our children learned not to risk taking any chances or hoping we would forget about a punishment because we had demonstrated that we would always follow through on any promise or threat. If they started to slip back into their old ways, all I had to do was pick up an item and walk out to the tree.

What is my point? We were teaching and disciplining our children from the time they were born. You can't start when your children are 7 or older. It's too late. As soon as they can comprehend teach your children what you want them to learn. Young children don't question results or reactions the way older ones will. Children need and want guidance. They want boundaries. They want to be loved. They want to feel safe. Don't be afraid to use some common sense and give them all of those things. Be consistent, fair and loving. All I can say is we raised two boys and three girls and it worked for each of them.

We also felt, and this is very important, that we could not expect our children to behave in a way that we were not behaving. That means if you don't want your children to use profanity, you can't use it. If you don't want your children to smoke, don't tell them not to smoke as you light up a cigarette. It makes no sense to expect your children not to drink if they see you drinking everyday.

The more your children respect and care about you, the more willing they are to imitate you. The more they will want to please you. Be careful what you are giving them to imitate. This doesn't mean you have to live over-protected, puritan-like lives. We didn't protect our children from alcohol, drugs, risqué movies or profanity. Unfortunately all of those exist in the world. It would serve no purpose pretending that they don't exist. We didn't give them long lectures. (Well maybe I did from time to time). We merely showed them by example they way we wanted them to be-by being that way ourselves. Sure there are vices everywhere, but your children won't need them if they have you.

Finally, we didn't go knocking down doors whenever we thought one of our children was being treated unfairly. We didn't rant and rave in a meeting or on the phone. We didn't run out and get a lawyer. We didn't start a crusade to get rid of the "offending" party. We ignored the vast majority of the situations and told our children they would have to get over it or get through it. As they got older our children no longer wanted or expected us to intervene on their behalf even if we were considering it. They simply got through the situation on their own.

In a few instances we did ask for an opportunity to clarify a situation or we wrote a letter to the person involved expressing our concerns and asking if there were some way we could all meet to see if there was some kind of a solution. That was it.

Our children, each at different times and in different ways, told us that the main reason they didn't do anything "bad" as they grew up was that they didn't want to hurt our feelings or disappoint us. Our family meant enough to our children that they didn't need as much acceptance from their peers. Consequently, they were able to resist certain offers or challenges without worrying about what their "friends" would say or think.

When the most important people in your children's lives are their own family members they will be much more confident and secure. To this day, even though our children range in age from 31 to 21 and live in four different states, they still call, email, and visit each other and us regularly. They are their own best friends. Three are college graduates and the youngest two are in the final year(s) of college. We still spend at least one holiday each year all together—now with their wives, boyfriends and girlfriends.

This may sound basic but this is something parents need to know more than ever. There is no doubt that parents can be the single most influential people in the lives of their children. That is the way it is suppose to be. That is the way it was meant to be. That is the way it needs to be. Having said that, permit me to express one of my greatest concerns.

Over the years I have noticed a dangerous trend being embraced by an ever increasing number of parents. In this group you will find parents who want to be "best friends" with their children. Being best friends with your children is great as long as you are not shirking your responsibility of being a parent first. If your main concern is being "liked" by your children you are going to make serious mistakes at critical times when it comes to raising them.

Then there are the parents who subscribe to the "belief" that kids are going to drink, smoke, do a little weed or other such behaviors no matter what, so as long as they do it at home or with a designated driver it's okay. They also believe that kids are going to have sex so as long as they are using "protection" it's okay. These are the parents who rent hotel rooms for their teens after the prom or other events so "at least they will be safe."

These parents know they can't really trust or control their children so the best they can do is "manage" them. Some of these parents may even drink, smoke and do drugs with their children. They feel it's better to do such things together so they and their kids can bond. Perhaps they don't see anything wrong in the behaviors to begin with.

To all of the parents I just described I want to say, "You are wrong." Maybe no one has ever told you that before. I have been dealing with your children for the past ten years and I am telling you now. You need to do more than manage your children—you need to raise them.

Too many parents today have made bad choices and have been bad role models when it came to their children. Too many others believe that they cannot be the most important influence in the lives of their children so they don't really try. The truth is all children first look to their parents for support and guidance. They don't know any better. If you believe something different, or have been told otherwise, you have been misled.

Why is it that we will listen to a doctor, a psychiatrist, a minister, a talk show host, a movie star, an "expert" or even a politician when they speak about raising children, but we don't seek advice from parents who actually raised successful children?

There are plenty of children and teens who do not drink, smoke, have sex or do drugs. They are living proof that children can indeed be raised that way. If you want to know how it's done, go ask their parents.

Here are the conclusions which resulted from a lengthy study undertaken to see how important parents were in the choices and decisions being made by their children.

Despite what parents may think, they have an enormous influence on their children's decisions about sex. More than two decades of high quality research, supplemented by recent public opinion polls, point to the same conclusion: the quality of parents' relationships with their teenagers can make a real difference in the decisions that their children make about sex. This Science Says brief makes the case that—even in a culture that bombards young people with conflicting and often-confusing messages about sex and pregnancy—parents remain powerful.

—(teenpregnancy.org)

Close parent-child relationships not only help protect young people from early sex and pregnancy, they also help teens avoid other such risky behaviors as violence, substance abuse, alcohol use, and school failure.

—(teenpregnancy.org)

There are so many powerful, negative forces and influences surrounding our children today it is more important than ever that the family structure be strong. Unfortunately, the once traditional family structure has never been weaker. There are fewer and fewer positive role models for children to emulate. It's more important than ever that parents are strong positive role-models.

If we don't somehow combat all the negative influences in our world what will prevent them from continuing to claim our children?

Someone is going to raise your children whether you like it or not. Make sure that someone is you.

Parents, the time has come to accept the idea that a good part of the way your children grow up is your responsibility. Whatever other factors and influences there may be do not remove the mantle of responsibility or the burden of accountability from your role in influencing the kind of people your children become.

Life's Lessons

I am fascinated by life's lessons. They are everywhere. Sometimes you can learn from something that happens to you. Other times you can learn by what happens to someone else.

I learned at an early age that I preferred to learn from what happened to other people. I am a little bewildered by people who insist on learning on their own. Some people actually seem proud when they proclaim, "I don't care what happened to him/her. I want to learn from my own mistakes." I always found that kind of thinking alarming.

For example, if a group of us were walking across a frozen lake and the ice broke under one of the other kids I did not need to walk over to the same area to see if the ice would break under me as well. Yet, for some reason, there are people who would walk right up to the same place, laughing all the way, and then fall in themselves. At such times, my laughter would immediately be replaced by the thought, "Are you kidding me!?" As most of us have learned, lessons we can learn by other people's mistakes are far less painful and embarrassing than those we learn on our own.

I want to share one little event which taught me a lesson I never forgot. This was the first time I learned to be aware of what was going on around me before I opened my big mouth. Since I was basically a shy lad I didn't learn this until I was about 12 years old.

It was a hot summer day and like any other hot summer day I was at the city swimming pool. One of my favorite activities at the pool was jumping off the high dive. It was about as thrilling an experience as I could find back in those days.

Well, one day I walked over to the bottom of the ladder leading up to the diving board and I noticed that sitting to my left, on two beach towels were two very cute girls. They were right at the edge of the grass, near the cement walk which went around the pool. I got the bright idea of impressing these young ladies by showing off on the high dive. Now you are probably expecting this story to end with me splashing in some embarrassing way into the water after jumping from the board. Oh no, I managed to find a way to humiliate myself before I even jumped.

As I stood at the bottom of the high dive, with several other kids above me on different rungs of the ladder leading to the top, I was contemplating which of my many impressive dives I would choose to impress and amaze the two cute girls sitting to my left.

A few seconds elapsed and I was able to climb to the first rung of the ladder. Now there were only about 5 other kids between me and the top of the diving board. I was getting excited. I couldn't wait to get to the top so I could unveil my diving prowess. However, the line wasn't moving. At least it wasn't moving at the speed to which I had become accustomed.

Finally after about a minute, I got to go up another rung. Well, at this pace the girls would be in high school before I got to the top. I became agitated. However, it was not in my nature to publicly express my agitation. So I waited. Finally it was time to go up another rung. There I was standing on the ladder, with the legs of the person in front of me staring me in the face.

I kept glancing at the girls hoping they wouldn't move from their towels. I started thinking, "What if they get up to go somewhere else just as I get to the top?" Panic was starting to set in. What was taking so long for this line to move? Again, I got to move up another rung. I didn't want the opportunity to impress the girls to slip through my fingers. I had to seize the moment.

As I moved up one more rung, I decided I had to take charge of the situation. As my frustration reached its breaking point, I yelled out,

"Hey move it up there!" I glanced over at the girls to see if they were impressed by my leadership and command of the situation. They were actually looking back at me!! Wow, this was turning out better than I had expected. Now maybe this line will get moving!!

Just as I finished shouting out my command, I was able to go up one more rung. Now the diving board was at my eye level. There was only one person between me and the person on the board. It was then I noticed the reason for the delay going up the ladder.

The boy who was now preparing to jump off the high dive was slowly hopping to the edge to jump off. Perhaps you were wondering why someone would be hopping across the diving board. Well, this young boy had only one leg. I had just yelled out, "Hey move it up there" to a young boy who was struggling to go up the ladder with one leg.

I couldn't muster the courage to even glance at the two girls. I waited for what seemed like an eternity for the one legged boy to jump. I could feel the red heat on my face. It was not the heat of the summer sun. It was that special warmth you only feel after making a complete fool of yourself. Finally the boy in front of me also jumped. Before he leaped into the water, however, he glanced back at me and shook his head. Ouch!

I had to wait another agonizing few seconds while I waited for the area under to board to clear. As soon as it did I ran across the board, jumped as far as I could. No fancy Olympic-style dives. No death-defying thrilling spins and twists followed by a perfect entry into the water. No, I just ran across the board and jumped out as far as I could.

I swam under water to the far side of the pool, got out, grabbed my towel, and quickly left the pool and went home. Lesson learned. Patience is not a burden, but rather a very good companion. Your own sharp tongue can just as easily cut you.

Signs of the Times

There is no doubt-these are complicated times. It seems as the negative influences on children grow more threatening, advances in technology have made access to these influences by our children easier than ever. There is little doubt that technological advances ranging from cell phones to the internet are amazing. The same can be said for the freedoms we are afforded in this country.

The price we are paying for these luxuries however is a loss of innocence and simplicity. Technology and freedom enable sinister people and irresponsible people to walk right into our homes. The influences we may deem inappropriate for our children are no longer down the street or across town. The people who preach hate, peddle drugs, sell sex, encourage mischief, and teach anarchy and terrorism are in our houses. They have moved right in and have become part of our families. They don't take up space or eat our food. They live in wires and cables and feed on our children.

As a parent you would be extraordinarily naïve to think your children have not seen pornography on your computer or on a friend's. There is also no doubt that they have been in one or more chatrooms talking about sex. They may themselves have been flirting with any number of other people in the room. There is a very good chance that your children have a "buddy list" comprised of not only friends from school, but also of people they "met" online. They probably "instant message" each other regularly. Topics often include "partying" and sex. How many hours does your child spend on the computer?

In addition there are many websites your children may not have visited—yet. Maybe one of their friends has though. These include sites dedicated to virtually every drug currently known. In these sites your children can learn what drugs are available, how to use them, where to get them, and how to make them. All the latest ways to abuse once innocent household chemicals or prescription drugs are also readily available.

There are numerous other sites that profess and promote racial hatred. They offer plenty of information and "reasons" why one race is better than another. Other sites preach "anarchy" and world "disorder". Still others are dedicated to the worship of Satan, witchcraft and demons. Gangs also have websites and use them for recruiting and promotion. Not to mention that anyone can find out anything they need to know if they want to build a bomb, another type of explosive or incendiary device.

In short, any information a person may want, no matter how deadly, destructive, perverted or prejudicial can easily be accessed using today's internet.

As dangerous as all of this information may be, it gets even worse. There is so much inaccurate information—especially about certain drugs, medications and explosives—that readers who don't know any better could end up seriously injured, ill or dead by believing what they read.

What is equally threatening is whether accurate or not, what one person discovers or figures out on Friday will be available worldwide by Saturday. There is no longer a long delay in information being spread from one area to another. Word of mouth is obsolete.

The internet poses a relatively new challenge today's parents must confront. This is a powerful force that parents in the past did not have to deal with. The internet in its own way is claiming victims every day.

What about trends in the more traditional sources of entertainment and information?

Movies, television and radio in the past often reflected the same values parents were teaching their children. "Controversial" or "delicate" topics were avoided.

For example, it wasn't so long ago when a husband and wife on a television program when shown in their bedroom, would be seen in separate beds—both wearing very appropriate pajamas. The whole idea of sex—even between married couples—was left to parents to handle. Naive and unrealistic—sure, but was that more harmful than what can be seen today?

In addition, families usually had only one TV. Parents and children would all watch the same program—together. There was limited programming. Some examples of programs that were on "back in the day" include, "Make Room for Daddy", "Leave It To Beaver", "Father Knows Best". "Walt Disney's Wonderful World of Color", and "Andy of Mayberry". I also remember watching "Flipper", "The Flintstones", "The Twilight Zone", "Outer Limits", "Dick Van Dyke" and "Gunsmoke". Of course there were numerous other programs but for the most part each of them had some kind of moral lesson.

The programs not teaching some kind of a moral were variety and entertainment oriented.

Shows such as "Ed Sullivan", "The Lawrence Welk Show", "Mitch Miller", "I Love Lucy", and "The Jack Benny Show" brought laughter and music into our homes. These programs too adhered to a certain standard. They were dedicated to originality, class and entertainment without trying to be provocative or shocking.

Even more recently shows like, "The Carol Burnett Show", "The Mary Tyler Moore Show", and "Bob Newhart" carried on the tradition of family fun and entertainment. In addition there were also entertaining shows with a moral like "Home Improvement" and "The Bill Cosby Show".

In the past there weren't many "mixed messages" inundating our children.

Isn't it laughable, yet very sad, that the epitome of a "bad" kid in the past was represented by the character of Eddie Haskell on the television show, "Leave It To Beaver?" Isn't it humorous remembering that Elvis Presley was once considered "threatening" because he wiggled his hips during his performances? Many of us remember when Elvis first appeared on "The Ed Sullivan Show", the cameraman was instructed to show him only from the waist up. Many more may remember how we were taken back by how "long" the Beatles' hair was when they too appeared on the "Ed Sullivan Show."

The history of families on television went from "Ozzie and Harriett" to "The Osbournes". Along the way we came to know the Cleavers, the Bradys, the Seavers and the Huxtables. Did this kind of innocence die because we wanted or needed to find something better? Perhaps we all wanted to become more sophisticated. We began to laugh at people who reflected "old fashioned" beliefs. Entertainers in greater numbers began to opt for being controversial, and provocative. Television decided to add "realism" to their programming.

Look at what can be viewed at any time of any day, on any day of the week on television now. Sex between married couples, unmarried couples, adults, teens and any other combination of partners is commonplace. We have long since abandoned the days of separate beds.

From network, to cable, and then to the internet, any adult or child can find plenty of graphic images depicting sex between men and women, multiple partners, same sex, older, younger, with animals, fetishes, live web cams, and more with virtually no effort at all.

Our children no longer have to wait until they are in college to go on "spring break". Now they can sit and watch it as soon as they are old enough to turn on the television. Isn't it wonderful that our elementary school children know what "body shots" are?

They also get to watch other programs in which females attempt to out-seduce each other trying to be the "lucky" one chosen by the male. There are any number of other "reality" programs where they can see "people just like them" randomly "hooking up" with each other.

Our children now get to watch primetime, network programs which continue to emphasize the stereotype of what is "beautiful". They see unhappy women who don't meet these "standards of beauty" choose to surgically alter themselves in an attempt to conform—on national television. One show, as you know, puts these surgically altered women in a contest and then tells all but one of them that they still don't measure up.

Another source of sexual imagery mixed with gratuitous violence can be found in today's video games. Like television programming, movies and the internet, even our games have jumped on the bandwagon of graphic images of sex and violence. There are supposedly systems in place preventing children from accessing the various sources of these explicit images. The reality is that these systems don't really work.

When you consider how sexually active and violent our teens and preteens have become is it possible that one factor contributing to this behavior is the proliferation of sexual and violent imagery in all forms of entertainment? Or is this "modern" behavior the result of some kind of natural evolution that would have occurred in spite of these "environmental" factors? I wonder what behaviors are waiting for us around the corner.

What about language? Is our tolerance of free speech at all time in all arenas adding to the acceptance profanity and of speaking improper English? Have we all just been worn down to the point we just don't care anymore? Look at the changes that have occurred in the past few decades in "acceptable" language.

It was once considered shocking and in bad taste to use words like, "damn" and "hell". People going to see the movie, "Gone With The Wind" for example waited for the big moment—not the burning of Atlanta or some other visually dramatic moment. The really big moment was when Clark Gable said, "Frankly my dear, I don't give a damn." That was considered scandalous!

Perhaps that was the beginning of what we see and hear today. Has moving so far away from that simplicity really been a good thing? Is there anyone today who is not aware of the language being spoken everyday on TV, in movies, in music, on playgrounds, in classrooms, and in our homes?

Speaking of music, does "art" reflect society or does it actually influence it? I think a case could be made to support both positions.

When I was growing up the vast majority of the songs that were popular were about dreaming, falling love, holding hands, breaking up, dancing and being misunderstood. Later, during the Viet Nam war, songs began to include lyrics protesting the war. There may also have been songs with "hidden" meanings or which made some veiled reference to sex or drugs, but for the most part they were pretty "tame."

Music basically reflected our lives and our lives reflected what we listened to and sang. Did our behaviors begin to change as music changed or did music change to reflect our behaviors?

Today, in many popular songs you will hear graphic lyrics about having sex and sexual positions. Other lyrics will refer directly to drinking, drug usage, and shootings. Many songs contain references to male and female body parts. Included in these songs are racial terms, lots of profanity, and demeaning and degrading terms for females. There are plenty of songs that celebrate the gang lifestyle. While numerous others songs contain dark imagery with lyrics glorifying evil and satanic references.

I could tell you some names of modern bands that would shock you by their graphic references to disease, death, and other morbid imagery. However, I will refrain so as not to give them any further recognition.

I am not referring to certain "underground" songs or bands. I am talking about bands and music your kids are listening to every single day. Songs have become so littered with obscenity and profanity that radio stations have to "bleep" or insert "dead air" to cover the offensive lyrics. I have heard songs on the radio which sounded like the radio was broken there were so many words missing.

Is there any need for me to describe what can be seen on stage today? When was the last time you witnessed what goes on during many live concerts either on stage or in the crowd? If today's children do as we did by imitating what they are seeing and singing, can today's "artists" be expected to accept some of the blame for the way our children are acting? Or do they get a "free pass" because they are "artist" merely pursuing their "art"? Will anyone ever accept responsibility for negatively influencing our children?

I think it is critical for parents to understand the length and breadth of the influences their children are facing. No more denial. No more rationalizing. Face the facts. Your children are inundated every single day by messages suggesting to them that sex, drinking, drugs, smoking, profanity and acting violently are acceptable. There are fewer and fewer role models or other influences telling them otherwise.

The absence of a strong message from you, in word and by example, showing them another way will leave them at the mercy of all the other influences in their lives. Once again the lesson is the same. There are people lining up to have access to your children. Make sure you know who they are letting in.

Professional Childhood

Whatever happened to the simple, pure pursuit of playing a game for fun? When was the last time you saw a group of kids on a dirt lot somewhere playing a game together just for the fun of it?

During the weekends and summers of my youth, not only did we play baseball for hours, using rocks, paper, tree branches and anything else we could find for bases, we also played imaginary games. On any given day we might be "army men" or scientists trapped on an island inhabited by monsters and dinosaurs. We were detectives, police officers and firemen. We were restaurants owners serving mud soup, mud pies, leaf salads and other fine cuisine. We played hide and seek almost every night until "the street lights came on". We did so with all the other kids in the neighborhood.

There were arguments about being "safe" or "out", or whose turn it was to be the captain of the troops or who got to make the mud pies and who got to use the fake cash register. We had to learn to compromise so the game could continue. We learned to use our imaginations. The better we imagined and created in our games, the more fun we had. To show you the depth of our imaginative skills, I remember spending an entire Saturday morning circling a small frozen pond, breaking off pieces of the clear ice pretending we were making glass for windows and jewelry.

We built "forts" with cardboard boxes. We made tents with an old blanket using tree branches and broom handles. We jumped rope, played "four square", hopscotch, tag (stoop tag, freeze tag and any number of variations). We made go-carts using old wagon wheels, and sleds using plastic and cardboard.

I remember how excited we would all be whenever one of the families in our neighborhood would get a new refrigerator, washer or tv. We would almost salivate looking at the cardboard box the item came in. To us, it meant we could move out of the old box and into the new one.

We would run through the sprinklers in the summer. Usually the parents would take turns letting us make messes of their yards. If you were lucky you knew a family who had a swimming pool. Where I grew up the family with the swimming pool had one of those wobbly pools with the metal siding that you set up above ground. They were a blast for a short time until we got tired of sitting in a small circular group surrounded by water filled with dirt and blades of grass.

Here is an activity that has definitely disappeared. As children, all of us would walk or ride our bikes everywhere we were allowed to go. The locations could be around the corner, down the street, through the woods, to school, to practice, to the vacant lot, you name it. We did so without ever having to worry about something bad happening to us. We could be gone for hours. We could leave our bikes wherever we dropped them and go play whatever game was on tap that particular day. When we were finished and ready to go home, our bikes would still be where we left them. I don't ever remember any of our parents worrying about us.

How was it possible for us to do so many things, and go so many places, with no supervision, or no cell phones without any dangers ever befalling us? We all know that those days are gone forever.

Here is a little sign, a ritual that to me symbolizes the kind of changes that have occurred in my lifetime. Many parents today feel that they need to accompany their children when they go "trick or treating" during Halloween—and rightfully so. Then upon arriving home they immediately inspect each piece of candy looking for some sign of contamination.

I certainly did both when my children were growing up. We had five children so this was no small undertaking. I would sit on the floor, dump out the bags (or pillow cases) one at a time and then examine each and every piece. I would look for loose wrappers, small pin holes, or anything that didn't seem right. If I had any doubt at all about the appearance of any of the pieces, I tossed them into a garbage bag.

None of our children ever complained. Looking back, it must have been excruciating for them. Then again, perhaps they never complained because they were all too aware of the reasons I was inspecting everything.

The only time our parents went through our Halloween candy when I was growing up was to see if there was something in the bag they wanted to eat. It never occurred to any of them they should check our candy for needles, razor blades, drugs or poison. In addition, I don't ever remember seeing any adults "trick or treating" with their children when I was a kid.

Are those days gone forever? If they are, did we replace them with something better? Isn't it a shame that we have arrived at a point in our history where there is so much potential for evil that we have to inspect candy given to our kids by our neighbors?

It's sad seeing innocent fun slowly disappearing during one's lifetime. Now there are only echoes of children playing baseball on the street or vacant lot. If you listen closely you might hear the faint sounds of children laughing as they zig and zag while playing tag. Listen again. Can you remember the sound of playing cards, held in position by old wooden clothes pins, fluttering in the spokes of bikes being ridden down the street sounding like make-believe motorcycles?

There are other sounds echoing too, but you will never hear them. They are being drowned out by the noise of car radios booming, engines roaring, horns honking, jet engines soaring, and sirens wailing.

Sometimes even those sounds can't be heard. Sometimes the only sounds that can be heard is the screeching and snarling of angry parents crackling through the air as they watch their children participating in an organized sport. To me this is the ugliest sound of them all.

We all know how important sports are in our American society. I think they have been elevated to a place where they are beginning to do more harm than good.

I played on many athletic teams as I grew up. My children played on numerous teams as they grew up. As a coach, I spent nearly 25 years involved in sports at every level other than collegiate. Oh the changes I have seen. If you have been involved for the past several years you have seen them too.

As a youngster I played baseball and football on our neighborhood or school league teams for years. I have searched every area of my memory and I cannot seem to find any recollections of parents ever yelling at their children, or at coaches or at officials. Perhaps they did, but I don't remember seeing it or hearing it.

I enjoyed winning and I was angry when we lost, but either way I got a bag of cheese flavored popcorn and a can of orange soda after each game. We had uniforms but nothing too flashy. I would wear my uniform t-shirt and cap all day and all night when we first got our baseball uniforms. I put on my shoulder pads and helmet as soon as I got home from the first football practice and ran through the house scoring touchdowns.

Our games were at modest fields either at a school or somewhere nearby. Often, after a game, I would hang out or maybe walk home with friends, some of whom played for the other team. My teammates and I usually used the bats and balls provided by the league. We had a choice of one or two bats and we used the same balls for the whole season. Occasionally one of the guys on the team would be lucky enough to get a brand new bat. Whenever any of us got a new bat we would always let the other guys use it too—but only for games.

Our parents had to pay a registration fee of maybe $20 or $30 and we were good to go. We looked forward to playing. I got nervous when I played. I didn't want to be the one who made a critical mistake, but it was still fun being out there with my friends. Our parents cheered when we did something good and were worried about us if we made a mistake.

Our coaches were adults who took the time and made the sacrifices necessary for us to be able to play. The officials were other parents who didn't have the time to coach, but wanted to help out at some of the games. I never saw one of my teammates or an opponent yell at an official. I saw adults tease an official but never berate him.

Gone are the days of innocence when it comes to youth/high school sports. A large percentage of today's young athletes who are playing on one or more sports teams are probably spending a fair amount of their childhood "on the road" with their "elite" travel teams. Many are also participating on a school or other local team. Team sports today have evolved to the point that they are almost professional.

Even at the age of 8, 9, and 10 years old boys and girls are playing on teams which are costing their parents hundreds if not thousands of dollars. Many have the latest equipment. They travel from state to state to play in the "important" tournaments. It is widely accepted today that any real athlete has to be on a "competitive travel team".

Parents of younger athletes feel that it will be a more valuable experience for their children if they compete against tougher teams at earlier and earlier ages. Playing on the "best" teams as the athlete gets older is considered essential. This is now accepted as the best way for an athlete to be seen by college coaches. If the athlete "stands out" enough, perhaps he/she will be rewarded with the all important athletic scholarship!

Youth/high school sports today have become big business. Sporting goods manufacturers have jumped on the bandwagon offering more and more products. Of course, the newer, better equipment keeps going up in cost. Companies are springing up, that for a fee, will assist parents in "marketing" their children to college coaches.

Many parents today have hired personal coaches for their sons and daughters to help give them "an edge." (Imagine if the same effort was being made and the same money was being spent to improve our children's academic prowess nationwide!)

I don't think it is any secret that in the world of youth/high school sports today you will find many parents who act more like agents than as a mom or a dad. Egos abound. These are the parents who are keeping an eye on what the sons and daughters of other parents are doing. They are constantly on the lookout for a "better" team, a "better" coach, and a "better" opportunity. Parents approach other coaches. Other coaches approach parents. "Deals" are made behind the backstop, in the stands, on the phone, or in a hotel room.

These parents can rattle off the statistics accumulated by their children like a sacred litany attesting to their athleticism and sports expertise. However, when asked about the names of their children's teachers or specific grades in specific classes they are hard pressed to come up with accurate answers. Why have so many parents forgotten what was once a priority?

In the past, parents put their children on teams so they could not only learn how to play the game, but more importantly to learn about discipline, teamwork and overcoming challenges. It was a way for everyone involved to have some fun and enjoy the experience together. It was a break from the rigors of school and chores. It was a pleasant break for the parents too. No matter what though, sports always took a backseat to academics. Those were the days.

Look at today's athletic contests. I am not referring to the antics of professional athletes or even those of collegiate athletes. As disappointing as many of the trends in professional and collegiate sports have become, I am more appalled by what is going on in youth sports.

Try finding a baseball, basketball, soccer, or softball game at which there are no parents howling and sneering at officials after virtually every call. Parents today will also yell out comments or insults directed at the coaches, other parents or even at the children playing—their own or someone else's.

Those who aren't screaming and berating the participants may be huddled together whispering to each other. They are pointing out all the mistakes being made by the coach and boasting about how much better they could do and how much more they know.

There are other parents who routinely subject their children to lengthy tirades in the car or at the dinner table criticizing the coach and the team. Still others constantly barrage their own children with lectures about their shortcomings and then force them to participate in additional "practices" at home with the angry, headstrong parent acting as the coach.

It is easy to find parents who never hold themselves accountable for their selfishness, immaturity, or poor sportsmanship. They have trampled upon anything meaningful and worthwhile. Teamwork, self-sacrifice, discipline, handling winning and understanding losing, putting others before self, exhibiting respect for one's opponent and just plain having fun, mean nothing to these parents. They do not care what kind of behaviors their children or their teammates may be exhibiting as long as they win and are on teams that keep winning.

Today many of our children are following in the footsteps of these parents. Between the behaviors they see in older athletes and that of their parents why should we blame them for the way they are acting?

So many young athletes today are not grateful or appreciative for the gift of health or for the opportunities to participate. How many "successful" youth teams have you seen with parents and athletes who act in a way that is more than obnoxious, it's actually disturbing? Why have so many parents "sold their souls" just to say their children are "winners"? When did the lessons once learned by participating in team sports become less important than the score?

It is sad that there are so many parents who see abuse of coaches, officials and other athletes as their right. Some see abusing coaches and officials as their responsibility! Why do none of the people ever feel shame?

As we all know there has been a dramatic increase in the number of incidents involving out of control parents at their children's athletic competitions. There seems to be so much anger involved in youth sports today.

I have seen parents yelling so forcefully that the veins in their foreheads were bulging out. Their faces were glowing red. Their nostrils flared and lips curled like snarling dogs. Fights are breaking out between parents in the stands or in the parking lot. Sometimes even the athletes are getting into fights during or after the "game." Officials are being ridiculed and even attacked. What is going on?

What kind of pressure are young athletes feeling and what effects will it have on them in the future? How many of these young athletes are only participating because they don't want to disappoint their agent-like parents? How many others simply have no choice? How many of them are having fun?

Look at how many injuries—physical and emotional—are occurring. How many young athletes have already had knee surgery or other medical procedures done on them? There are many athletes in their teens who have quit, or want to quit team sports, because of the pressure, the unrelenting commitment and the lack of fun they experienced in the world created by these crazed parents and "win at all cost" coaches. What will youth sports be like in another five or ten years if these trends continue?

Sadly, few of the parents and coaches creating the corrupt atmosphere found in so many youth sports today will ever accept the responsibility or apologize for the damage they are doing. In their obsessed minds they see themselves as heroes championing the cause of winning at all cost, while ensuring their sons, daughters or their team get everything that's coming to them.

It is no longer about lessons learned or being part of a team. It is now only about individual statistics, playing time, showing off, "standing out" and trophies. The team is merely the vehicle that is used to further one's opportunities, reputation and "career."

Many of these agent parents are usually blind when it comes to the abilities of their children. Ask any college or high school coach how many times they have been approached in their off season by a parent touting the skills of their son or daughter only to find out later that the "star" athlete was average at best.

One of the really damaging effects these parents have had is actually on their own children. These parents are so wrapped up and blinded by their personal obsessions that they convince their children they are stars. Consequently these child stars begin to act the way they think stars are suppose to act. They are encouraged every step of the way by their proud agent parents.

These are the young athletes with the fancy wrist bands, head bands, fancy shoes and the latest sunglasses and equipment bags. These stars and their parents often arrive late for games or practices so they can make an entrance. These families are well known in the world of little league and other youth sports. Believe it or not they exist in high school sports as well. They live in a fantasy world never realizing they are the targets of ridicule and jokes by all those who encounter them. They are not only disruptive, they are constant sources of conflict the team has to overlook and the coach has to deal with.

Unfortunately for these children there comes a time when they will inevitably experience disappointment and even shock when reality comes knocking. At some point in their careers these young "stars" find out their parents were wrong. They weren't special! Whether in high school, on a travel team or in college, sooner or later, these mislead, pampered prima donnas find out their parents have made fools out of them.

The results can be very traumatic. Not only are they embarrassed, their self-esteem and self-confidence are shaken. I have seen time and time again when children who had been mislead and misinformed by their public relations parents struggled mightily when reality stared them in the face. For some reason, there parents were no where to be found.

Make no mistake about this; these same behaviors are not restricted to athletics. They can also be easily found in cheerleading, high school marching bands, high school orchestras and even in school plays.

Realistically, none of the parents or children guilty of these behaviors will ever understand that this is about them. Few will ever learn, until it is too late, that trophies, ribbons and headlines matter little when you can no longer hide behind the athlete you were and you are forced to exist as the person you are.

It's too bad that all the families dragging their children across the country, from one tournament to another, won't realize until it's too late that they should have bagged the team and the tournaments. It would have been so much better if they had just spent the time traveling as a family simply to see the sights and enjoy each other's company while they had the chance.

Remember, once your children have grown up, you will never get another chance to be a part of their childhoods. They will never get another chance to have a childhood. Childhood is a fleeting moment in time not a profession.

Education—"Leave No Criminal Behind"

"Leave no child behind". What a beautiful concept. Let's see to it that every child will be included. Let's embrace all children and give them each the time and effort they deserve. Let's educate them and find places for all of them in our classrooms. What a beautiful world.

When was the last time you spoke to a teacher or administrator about this concept? You would be hard pressed to find one who supports this idea. Why?

Remember when students had to sit in class and behave? The younger you are the more likely it is that you will answer that question with a, "No."

However, there once was a time when all students sat quietly for the whole class period and listened to the teacher. Many would ask questions. There were disciplinary consequences for any behaviors that were inappropriate. If some kind of issue existed between a teacher and a student, the student's parents would side with the teacher. The times have changed.

Today the students who are sitting in class and who are trying to learn have to do so in many cases in spite of other students who routinely disrupt what the teacher is trying to teach. Students who are "under the influence", who are undisciplined or just plain rude, monopolize many classrooms today.

In our attempt to "leave no child behind" we have created a safe haven for every child—even the bad ones. Yes, I said it. Believe it or not, there are bad students today. They are bad in the sense that they haven't been brought up well. Bad in the sense that they have no interest in getting an education and enjoy disrupting the attempts of others trying to do so. Bad in the sense that they only "attend" school to be with their boyfriends, girlfriends or with their other friends. Bad in the sense that they are experts at using the system to get what they want.

These students have learned that there are few, if any, consequences for their behaviors. Other than incidents of extreme violence or weapon possession the system is setup to keep letting students come back to school time and time again after being suspended repeatedly for other offenses. There is little the disruptive students can do to get themselves expelled.

Administrators are reluctant to suspend and expel students because it might affect the dropout rate at their respective schools. Administrators also have to worry about the consequences they may face when they do discipline a student. It is not unusual for any disciplinary action to be questioned or resisted by irresponsible, finger-pointing parents. Administrators are routinely threatened with lawsuits by these "enabling" parents. Of course there is always an attorney who is only too happy to come to their aid.

There was a time when the actions taken by a teacher or administrator were always supported by parents. Lawsuits were virtually unheard of. Why did this change? Have teachers and administrators become so derelict in their duties that parents and students had no recourse but to seek legal remedies?

Or, have we become more irresponsible, and less willing to accept the consequences of our actions and those of our children? Every school has a teacher or two who perhaps could do a better job. I am sure the same is true about administrators. But what about the students? Why are so many causing problems or simply not motivated to learn? Whatever happened to "reading, writing, and 'rithmetic"? What about the parents?

I have dealt extensively with students who had been disciplined for a rules or policy violation of some kind. It is becoming increasingly rare that the student and parent both apologize for, or even admit to, the wrongdoing. It is more likely that they are going to make an excuse or some kind of accusation.

Some parents will accuse the teacher or some other adult for being the person in the wrong. If their son or daughter was found to be in possession of a controlled substance for example, they are more concerned about the legality of the search than they are about their son or daughter being in possession. If their son or daughter was involved in a fight they are more interested in what punishment the other student is going to get. If the student isn't going to class, it's because the teacher isn't interesting enough. If the student is disruptive the school has to make adjustments to accommodate the individual needs of that student.

There are numerous students today who have a completely separate plan and an entire support staff to service their "individual needs". (On a side note, I find it curious that students who are considered incorrigible, or have been "diagnosed" with certain learning disabilities or disorders, the ones who mouth off, show up late for class, don't do their work, as well as numerous other inappropriate behaviors, are always on time for lunch, never miss a "passing period" and always manage to catch the bus which takes them home from school everyday).

It seems that in our attempts to leave no child behind we are actually leaving many children behind. Who are these children? Children who have to fend for themselves while all the attention is being given to the trouble-makers. Children whose education is watered down to accommodate the weakest link. Children whose classroom experience includes numerous interruptions and distractions. Children who are being taught by teachers who are burnt out, fed up, or frustrated by the system. Children who will never be taught by some really great teachers because the teachers opted to take early retirement or chose another field so they could free themselves from the current educational environment.

Here's another thought. Public education is just that—public. That means that we are paying for it. It's a public program. Why are there no minimum requirements for a student to continue in the program? By that I mean, why are students with GPAs of 0.00 or 0.089, for example, allowed to stay in the school? Wouldn't it make more sense to have some kind of requirement? Do you think requiring every student who wants to take part in our public educational system to maintain some type of minimum GPA—perhaps a 1.0 (D average) would be appropriate?

A common argument against "kicking" students out of school is that they will be out on the streets causing some kind of trouble. Also, it is believed that once students are discouraged or prevented from attending school that they will fall behind and eventually just drop out anyway.

My question is this. Why is it better to keep such a student in school? This amounts to babysitting and nothing more. In addition we are basically saying that we don't want that youngster on the streets where he/she may cause trouble. We prefer to put them in a classroom with the students who are trying to learn where they can cause trouble. Perhaps this makes sense to you. I, for one, cannot see the logic.

If you are a parent of a student who is actually trying to learn, your child is being shortchanged by this policy. In my opinion, parents of students who are bearing the consequences of the policies which limit the educational experiences and opportunities of their children should be more demanding.

Why do we give so much preferential treatment to the troublemakers? Ask your son or daughter if they know of a "student" who is constantly in trouble, who doesn't want to learn, and yet is continuously permitted to remain in their class and at their school. Ask your son or daughter if their classes are disrupted by such students. Ask your son or daughter if their teachers ever get frustrated or have less time to teach because they have to deal with such students. If so, why is this being tolerated? Why is this okay? Why aren't you doing anything about it?

If a student doesn't maintain a minimum GPA or is "disciplined" a certain number of times they should have to face real consequences.

Perhaps performing community service after school would be something to consider. Students who did not meet the requirements for receiving their free education should have to work in an after school community service program until the next grading period at which time their grades would be re-evaluated.

They could pick up litter, remove graffiti, weed the medians of our streets, clean up our parks, and any number of other beneficial tasks. Failure to attend the after school program would result in their removal from the public educational system. This is just an idea, a suggestion.

Certainly there would be a number of factors to consider. I am just trying to start the ball rolling, to change some longstanding attitudes and practices. I am sure there are other ideas or suggestions which would surface if we made protecting the real students more of a priority.

If parents in each community, each school district, each city, and each state were holding the policy-makers more accountable for plans that allow violent, disruptive, disrespectful or unmotivated students to prevail perhaps real changes might finally result.

These failing policies are not supported by most teachers or administrators anyway. They have been forced upon them by "experts" who have lost touch with what is really taking place in our schools today. Many of these "experts" are not even in the classroom. Some never have been in one. They are driven by numbers and dollar signs. They are more concerned with image than education. They want to avoid lawsuits rather than encourage excellence and integrity.

Another question I have is why are so few students "held back" today? I don't know about you, but when I was growing up there was always at least one child in class who didn't pass the previous year. It is almost unheard of for a student to be held back today. There are several reasons for this.

First, parents won't permit it. It's too embarrassing. The student and parent(s) would simply blame the teacher and demand satisfaction.

Another reason is that most teachers, when faced with failing a student or passing him/her will opt to pass them. This is especially true for the problem student who is disruptive. This is also the case with underachieving students who keep getting passed on to the next level because it's just plain easier than "proving" they should be held back.

Today there are so many "headaches" associated with actually failing a student that it makes doing so more traumatic than it's worth. Don't blame the teacher or the system. Much of the blame should fall on the student and his/her parents.

Let's face it. Education is taken for granted in this country. It's not appreciated or respected the way it once was. Not so long ago it was considered to be a privilege. Now many students feel it's a burden, a necessary evil. Students are less willing to study subjects they feel they won't need. More and more of them are opting to get G.E.D.s, or go to "charter schools." Across the country there a millions who are just dropping out. Why is this happening?

One major reason is students today lack discipline and drive. They want things to be easy. They want to be "entertained" not educated. Parents seem to be less demanding as well. I am speaking in general terms of course. However, there is no denying all of what I just described. So there has to be some explanation. Parents and students have to accept most of the blame. The reason is that they are the educational system.

If parents aren't satisfied with public education, if they are tired of the trends which have produced the results we are now getting they can change things. There is one fact about education that cannot be disputed. That is the loudest, most persistent parents get what they want.

Parents also need to be more supportive of their children's teachers. They need to get involved, but not interfere with education. Quite simply this system isn't working. I am trying to let you know, so hopefully there will be enough parents of deserving students whose demands for some explanations and accountability will finally be heard.

If you are still not convinced, ask yourself this. What does it mean that today many middle schools and high schools across America need police officers and other security personnel on their campuses to maintain order and provide some level of safety? Others also have metal detectors and/or security cameras.

This was unheard of for the first 180 years or so of public education in this country. Why has that changed so drastically in such a short time? The behaviors necessitating the need for security are not natural evolutionary changes. These behaviors were not pre-ordained or unavoidable.

The reason schools now need police and security personnel is because so many of our students are engaging in criminal activity. Drugs are abundant. Violence is common. Theft is routine. Vandalism is rampant. Gangs are ever-present.

According to the National Household Survey on Drug Abuse, in the 2002 more than 5 million youths engaged in serious fighting at school, while 4 million took part in group on group fighting. In 2002 we didn't have hundreds or thousands or even hundreds of thousands of students involved in violence. There were over FIVE MILLION students involved in fighting.

The list of inappropriate non-criminal activity is even longer. This list includes lack of respect, temper tantrums, cheating, rudeness, boisterousness, and disobedience. Most students are children. They are your children. Many of them have been so poorly raised and trained that we now need security officers in our schools to protect staff and other students from them. Yet these are the same students we don't want to leave behind.

With so many educated, highly trained, experienced people involved in our educational system you would think that education would be virtually problem-free. The fact is we don't need anymore experts. We don't need any more studies or theories. What we do need is more discipline, more consistent consequences and a much better partnership between parents and teachers. What we need is to start leaving some children behind.

Drugs/Alcohol

Drugs, in my opinion, are the biggest, most insidious threat to America. This includes prescription drugs, illegal drugs, household cleaners and solvents, and alcohol. Legal or not, these substances are doing more damage to our country, especially to our children, than any other force or threat. There are so many layers to this problem, it is often avoided. The problem just seems too overwhelming.

Not only are the effects of drug usage in America negatively impacting every American, our overall need for instant gratification, our tendency to want to escape, our lack of self-discipline and the availability of drugs/alcohol all combine to make this the single most destructive force in our society.

We understand threats posed by terrorists. We understand natural disasters. We rally to our own defense when faced with either. For some reason, however, we have tolerated a force even more deadly and more relentless. This merciless tyrant, this child-killer, this evil, walks amongst us everyday. It is embraced by many, fought by others and ignored by the rest. The list of casualties, the cost, the suffering, the resulting crime and the victims of that crime cannot be fully measured. Drug abuse has become part of our lives and part of our deaths.

Maybe it's time to review our perception of drugs and alcohol and their usages. I realize that this will not be a very popular notion. Alcohol is found in virtually every area of our society. It's legal. It's accepted. Yet look at how many deaths occur each year which are directly the result of its use. Look at how many relationships, marriages, families, and careers are destroyed because of this accepted, readily available commodity.

Now "binge drinking" has become common at high school parties and on college campuses. Our children are using funnels and tubes to consume large quantities of alcohol in a matter of seconds.

Here is the sobering truth about alcohol. There is a very good chance that your children either already have or one day will drink this way. At the very least they will be standing in the group cheering on someone else who is. This is just the tip of an iceberg of destruction.

Let's look a little closer at what is going on with the abuse of alcohol. If these numbers are not a "wake-up call" then we are not just asleep, we must be unconscious! Here are the results of information gathered by the National Household Survey on Drug Abuse:

In 2001, almost half of Americans ages 12 or older reported being current drinkers of alcohol (48.3%). This translates to 109 million people. This is an increase from 46.6% or 104 million in 2000.

20.5% of persons ages 12 and older participated in binge drinking.

In the age group of 12 to 17-17.3% used alcohol in the month of the survey. This is up from 16.4% in 2000.

In 2001 10.1 million people ages 12 to 20 reported drinking in the month of the survey. Of these 6.8 million were binge drinkers. 2.1 million were "heavy" drinkers.

In 2001 25.1 million people ages 12 to 20 drove at least once under the influence of alcohol.

In 2001 the percentage of people surveyed who drove under the influence of alcohol was 11.1%. In 2000 that percentage was 10%. (So much for "Don't Drink and Drive").

Unfortunately the use and abuse of alcohol is so widespread and so accepted it would take a monumental effort over a period of years to change things.

Drugs are no different. We all know what drugs are doing to our society. While some people want to see some or all of them legalized, others stand firmly against them. There are many others who are simply confused or uncertain about what to think or feel. The problems with drugs are so overwhelming it feels like there will never be an effective solution.

Here is an even scarier thought. This alone should be reason enough to start changing our acceptance and perception of drugs. Established substances like marijuana have become even more potent than when it was first introduced. Also newer drugs are being "discovered" virtually everyday. The threats that drugs pose are actually getting worse.

"Designer" drugs like MDMA (Ecstasy or "X"), GHB, Rohypnol, Ketamine and others have become more easily attainable. Consequently their use has been steadily increasing in the past few years. For instance, according to the 2002 National Survey on Drug Use and Health, more than 10 million people have tried ecstasy at least once.

GHB and Rohypnol use is also on the rise. These are the most common "date rape" drugs. They will render a person (almost always a female) helpless and therefore unable to fend off sexual assault. The victim may have no recollection of the assault because one side effect is amnesia.

These drugs only came into prominence in the early 1990s. However, their use in sexual assaults increased so rapidly that Congress passed the "Drug-Induced Rape Prevention and Punishment Act of 1996" in an attempt to curb their use.

This law states, *"The Drug-Induced Rape Prevention and Punishment Act of 1996 (Act), 21 U.S.C. Sec. 841(b)(7), provides criminal penalties of up to 20 years imprisonment for any person who distributes a controlled substance, such as Rohypnol, to a person with the intent to commit a crime of violence, including rape."* Shouldn't we all be more alarmed that such a law was even necessary?

One measurement of the explosive growth of GHB (another "popular" date rape drug) can be seen in the amount of "emergency department episodes" related to its use. In 1994 there were 55 such episodes reported. In the year 2000 the number of reported episodes rose to 4,969. This number dropped to 3340 in 2001, but it's easy to see the threat these drugs are posing. (*NIDA Research Report Series*).

In addition prescription pain relievers such as oxycontin, once ignored, suddenly became so widely abused that the frequency of robbery and theft to obtain this drug forced many pharmacies to discontinue its availability. In 1999 an estimated 4 million people were currently using prescription drugs non-medically. In that same year, The National Household Survey on Drug Abuse determined that the sharpest increases in new users of prescription drugs for non-medical purposes was found in 12 to 17 and 18 to 25 year-olds.

Items that have been available on the shelves of grocery stores and drug stores for generations must now be kept in secure places. For example, cold remedies containing dextromethorphan (DXM) which is found in Coricidin and Robitussin, for example, are also becoming abused more than ever. The effect of overdosing on this drug creates different "plateaus of hallucinogenic highs". Children are consuming large doses of these once harmless remedies at an alarming rate right under their parents' noses.

One of the newest drugs that is being abused is called, opioid fentanyl. This is a narcotic painkiller that resembles a small lollipop. It was designed to ease the pain of cancer sufferers. On the street this drug is called, "perc-a-pops." In the year 2000 hospitals reported 576 cases of non-medical uses of fentanyl products. The number of reports in 2002 rose to 1506. It is likely that the abuse of this drug will continue to rise as its popularity spreads.

Sniffing paints and cleaners, also known as "huffing" has risen dramatically in just the past few years. One study released in March of 2004 states that 1 out of every 5 children has admitted to huffing at least once by the time they reach the eighth grade. Some students stated they began huffing at the age of 6!

Clearly drugs of all kinds and variations are not only becoming increasingly available, the willingness of people to abuse them at younger ages is also growing. In addition, easy access to the internet has made "sharing" information about drugs, including how to make, obtain, and use them a daily activity for many teens. There are even websites dedicated to the promotion of specific drugs of choice.

Many of the most popular sites contain misinformation and medical inaccuracies which make these sites particularly dangerous. Information about newly "discovered" drugs or new uses of old drugs, as well as false information, is now spread instantly around the world. Consequently, it no longer takes months or years for the popularity of a drug to grow. Unfortunately this is also true about the speed at which false information is also spread. Imagine the future health issues that are awaiting us when today's drug users become tomorrow's parents.

Maybe we can't "see the forest for the trees." Perhaps most Americans didn't realize the direction we are heading when it comes to drugs and alcohol. Maybe we did but just looked the other way because the problem is so pervasive. I suppose there may be any number of Americans who won't feel that any of this is a problem. Drugs and alcohol are not necessarily seen by everyone to be the threat that I feel they are. What do you think?

If the statistics weren't scary enough, think about the number of crimes, illness, death and damage which are the direct result of people's use of drugs and alcohol. Seriously, think about that. How many deaths have resulted each year of drug users or victims of drug users? Think about the number of rapes which resulted from date rape drugs or alcohol usage. Sexually transmitted diseases, pregnancies, abortions, and birth defects are also affected.

I wonder how much money and other personal possessions were taken last year for reasons related to drugs and alcohol. How has all of this impacted law enforcement, our courts and our prisons? The domino effect that drugs and alcohol have caused is toppling virtually every structure we have put in place to provide a better quality of life for us all.

Just imagine what this country would be like if humans had enough discipline to avoid drug and alcohol usage in the first place. Consider the dramatic impact that would have in every area of our society. It is horribly tragic that so much of what is helping to destroy this country is the result of human beings willingly ingesting substances they are free to avoid. We now live everyday with mayhem that we are inflicting on ourselves.

Is the state of our society a natural step in the evolutionary process of human beings? Was this kind of behavior inevitable? Or does it represent some kind of a failure of our society and our frailty as human beings? You would think that as humans evolved behaviors that are so clearly self-destructive would eventually be phased out.

Why then are we still so willing to breathe in smoke and ingest chemicals and other substances which are so harmful to us? Using the science fiction analogy, imagine how human beings in America would look to aliens from another planet. I don't know if they would scratch their heads trying to make sense out of our behaviors, or laugh hysterically at our lack of intelligence and our willingness to self-destruct.

Given all the information we have about the deaths, illnesses, crimes and costs associated with drug and alcohol abuse why is it that those who speak out against their use are often looked down upon? If the same statistics were the result of actions being taken by terrorists against our country we would be rising up en masse to take action against their evil-doings. If that would be our reaction to a terrorist act, why don't we respond to the drug problem that way? Is the death and destruction we are experiencing any less real? Are drug dealers less sinister or doing less harm than terrorists? What about the fact that much of the activity of terrorist groups and of course drug cartels is being funded by Americans with the money we are spending on drugs?

The time has come for us to change our attitudes, our perceptions and our tactics when it comes to the drug/alcohol problem in America. There is nothing "casual" or "recreational" about the impact drugs/alcohol are having on our country. Millions of people will probably disagree with this assessment, perhaps laughing at the futility of trying to change something so accepted and so entrenched in our society. They are adding to the destruction.

Maybe the problem is just too overwhelming to solve. Perhaps the net result of drug and alcohol use and abuse, when coupled with the effects of smoking and obesity, will eventually overtake us all. Maybe there is a death knell ringing in the distance that is falling on deaf ears.

These trends are not going to stop themselves. Think about that the next time you see someone joking about getting high or being drunk while everyone else around them laughs hysterically.

Crime

It is shocking to me that virtually every American has been a victim of some kind of a crime. If for some reason, you have not been, you will be. If you only suffered some materialistic loss you are lucky. Most of us have had something stolen or vandalized. We are the fortunate ones. There are so many others not so fortunate.

Is there any need to review the number of families in our country who wake up each day mourning the loss of someone they love? Think about that. How many parents have had a child taken from their lives?

Imagine the first 30 seconds of every, single morning when a parent whose child was killed begins to awake. The realization and pain of their loss is the first thought awaiting them. It's heartbreaking knowing there are so many good people whose days always begin that way. How many more little caskets will we have to build?

America leads the world in the number of homicides. Are murder, mutilations, and other such crimes something a free society just has to tolerate because it comes with the territory? Look at some of the horrific crimes which are no longer considered unusual. This is most disheartening when the crimes involve children.

Surely we are all aware of some of the heinous crimes occurring everyday against children. They include: parents torturing, drowning, shaking, and beating, their own children—or someone else's. What about raping their children? It's still considered sad today, but it no longer is considered shocking. We live with serial killers, serial rapists, crimes involving cannibalism, sexual torture, kidnapping, and child pornography. Domestic violence is an everyday occurrence.

It's horrifying to me imagining what the last minutes or hours of any victim of violence must have been like. It's a reality much easier to forget. Did the victims close their eyes while they were being attacked? Did their fear overpower their pain? Did they know they were going to die before they actually did? Did they die with thoughts of their loved ones flashing in their minds? Were they hoping that death would come soon?

These may seem like inappropriate questions to you, but those questions bring into focus the horror that is surrounding us. I think too many of us have become jaded when it comes to any tragedy that doesn't directly affect us. What we are forgetting is that every tragedy does affect us. We just shut it out.

Why is it no longer safe for our mothers, wives, sisters and children to walk alone—even in daylight? Why do so many criminals have to be so sinister, so brutal and so unremorseful? Why is it getting to be common for a police officer who is describing a crime scene to say something like, "I have been on the force for 25 years and I have never seen a crime scene as disturbing as this one."?

What about all the crimes of rape, molestation, violence and intimidation that aren't even being reported? How many women and children are living today in fear, while the pain and remorse caused by some despicable adult or teenager is suffocating the joy and peace from their lives? The truth is you are either a victim or you know a victim of this type of crime. There will be a whole new "batch" of victims tomorrow so be prepared.

We are being told that crime is on the decline in America and has been for the past decade. I have no reason to doubt the statistics. As we all know, however, statistics are only as good as the people reporting and gathering them. Even as I write this there are investigations being launched to determine how widespread crime statistic manipulation has become.

Let us also remember that there are many police departments across the country, which for various reasons, do not receive any federal funds. These departments are not required to report their statistics to the Department of Justice. None of the crimes committed in the jurisdictions of these departments are included in those the Justice department's reports.

So perhaps the numbers we are using to indicate there has been a decrease in crime during the past 8 to 10 years is more the result in the way these numbers are gathered. Even if crime were truly declining, why do most people feel less safe today?

What about the nature of the crimes being committed? How did we go from "rumbles" to drivebys? Is it inherent in the human being to "evolve" in this way or is it the result of the influences our society has tolerated or even embraced?

Here are some examples of recent crimes making the news. Are these crimes just isolated occurrences or are they a reflection of the society that we are shaping?

Son kills 78 yr old mom with an axe, chops up body parts and burns them one by one.

Young mother leaves 14 month old daughter in the snow with a knife sticking out of her back. The young girl was still alive sitting alone in the snow when found.

12 & 13 year old boys rape 10 year old student in the school's bathroom.

Man murders his 67 yr old mother. Her body is found in a tub with her throat slashed several times and her pubic area cut out.

Father sells young teenage daughter to two men in exchange for "crack". She is beaten and raped by both and left behind a dumpster.

Mother kills 2 of her children by bludgeoning them to death with a rock "to please God".

Father kills 10 family members, stacks bodies in piles. He also fathered his own grandchildren.

A mother and her two daughters, one 19 and one 13, join in a group beating of a 12 year old girl at the 13 year old girl's birthday party. Three other girls, 13, 14 and 15 years old also participated in the beating of the 12 year old. The girl who was beaten was in a coma for three weeks and is facing a life suffering from brain damage. She was beaten by the woman and her daughters for kissing a male party guest who was considered to be the 13 year old girl's "boyfriend".

A 12 year old boy uses his bare hands to strangle an 8 year old girl who was riding her bike to a friend's house. He then concealed her body in some tall weeds in a nearby wooded area.

Do you remember or have you heard about the kidnapping of Charles Lindbergh's infant son? It made headlines around the world. It shocked, horrified and devastated the people of that day. When the infant's dead body was finally found the world came to a standstill. Mourning and prayers for the family spread across the entire planet. What a tragedy.

Have you ever wondered why none of the crimes I listed above created anything close to the same reaction as the Lindbergh kidnapping? All of them together did not create the same reaction. We have not only produced the type of people who would commit such crimes, we ourselves have become more "accepting" and less outraged because of the regularity such crimes are now committed. Who is building this society anyway?

The Un-Legal system

The only reason we need courts, lawyers and judges is because so many people are inherently dishonest. Imagine what it would be like in our society if every single person simply chose to honest and law-abiding. Look at what that would mean.

There would be no crime, no lies, and no cheating. No one would steal from you, or mislead you. There would be no corrupt politicians, judges, lawyers or police officers. Big corporations and small shops alike would be deception-free places of business. Employers would not cheat employees and employees would not cheat employers. Companies would not cheat their customers.

There would be no kickbacks, no insurance fraud, welfare cheating or shoplifting. Spouses would not cheat on each other. There would be no drug usage because drugs are illegal. Alcohol would still create some problems, but at least there would be no underage drinking (or smoking) because that would be illegal as well.

There would be no need for courts, judges, lawyers and juries because whenever a ruling was needed, let's say for some kind of an accident, each person involved would just tell the truth about how it all happened. The guilty party would just admit it. The injured party would only ask for what was actually lost—nothing more. Simple, basic honesty would replace virtually every trial.

All of this and more would be possible if people were simply honest and law-abiding. What makes this so sad, tragic even, is dishonesty is a choice! No one is born dishonest. That is something we choose to be as we grow up. Dishonesty today is an epidemic.

Think of how "normal" it is for people to lie—even little "white" lies. Cheat on your taxes? Who amongst us claims every single dollar earned? Call and cancel that dinner engagement because your spouse was "ill"? Have you ever told someone answering the phone to "Tell them I'm not home."? Ever walk out of the store and then notice the cashier neglected to ring up the deodorant? Do you go all the way back to correct it? Someone gives you the incorrect change, an extra dollar, do you give it back? Everytime?

It starts here and then ends with people pleading, "Not guilty" to a crime they are fully aware they committed. Look around you, or even at you. Imagine our world, or even our country, if it were inhabited by people who simply chose to be honest all the time. Yep, the reason we need all the courts and lawyers we have now is because there are so many dishonest people.

One reason for this is because there are so many unscrupulous lawyers who justify dishonesty everyday. These same lawyers see truth as a threat to their chances of winning the case. Truth is an obstacle that must be overcome in order to win. Lawyers insist that their clients get a "fair" trial and then immediately proceed to pull as many tricks, misdirections and shenanigans as they can to make the trial as unfair as possible. Many lawyers are the epitome of "enablers."

Lawyers proudly proclaim that they are the defenders of the law, the seekers of justice. Yet we all know, as do they, the law has been made a sham, a rouse by these pompous, pontificating, perverters of all that is just.

Overweight? No problem. A "lawyer" will sue the people who make food. Charged with your 5th DUI? No problem. A lawyer will get you off by pointing out that the police officer put the wrong date on the police report. Kill somebody? Don't worry. Your lawyer will justify it because of the extenuating circumstances in your life—and—point out all the mistakes the police department made during the investigation. Rape somebody? Don't sweat it. As soon as your lawyer is through humiliating your already traumatized victim you will be free to do it again. Lose your paycheck at the casino? Stop worrying. Your lawyer will sue the casino for enticing you to spend it all.

No matter what you do, no matter how irresponsible you are, how illegal your actions are or how devastating your crime may have been, regardless of how much evidence there is against you, you will always be able to find a lawyer who will put the blame where it belongs—on anyone and everyone other than you.

If you were to listen to the average defense attorney or other lawyers you would think that in this country an astounding 90% of people charged with a crime were actually innocent! 90% of our criminals were falsely accused! It sure is a good thing we have so many lawyers protecting all of these falsely accused innocent men and women!

Perhaps you will find yourself with a mediocre lawyer. You are worried about actually being found guilty of the crime you committed. Relax. The odds are you will be given a very stern lecture and then be put on probation by some judge who has lost all touch with reality. To a frustrated observer of our current legal system it appears there is a secret contest going on between judges to see who can hand out the most lenient, ineffective sentences.

Here is some advice. If you have your choice of being a criminal or a victim, choose criminal. It will be much easier on you. (I should delete that because some lawyer will sue me for being the reason his/her client committed some crime). Oh yeah, don't forget to get a lot of media attention! The more media you can get, the better your lawyer will be. The best lawyers always go where the media is—regardless of the client's guilt or innocence.

Here is another thought to consider. For many violations our courts decide if a person is guilty and then impose a sentence. In this respect courts are like parents and the people on trial are like children (in more ways than one). Even if a jury is doing the deciding, the idea is that consequences are being determined for someone's inappropriate actions.

I believe the same principles that apply in raising children should apply in the handling of someone who commits a crime. If the legal system consistently handed out strict, uncompromising sentences, with no stalling, or lawyer tricks tolerated, there would be a measurable impact on the amount of crime.

It seems to me that courts have gone overboard in focusing on the "welfare" of the criminal. It's good to try each case on its own merits. However, judges don't seem to take into account the "deterrent" aspect of sentences. When this aspect of sentencing is ignored or minimized it actually increases the likelihood that the criminal will re-offend. Even worse, light sentences such as probation and community service are perceived by others involved in crime or contemplating criminal activity as encouragement to proceed.

After all if the only consequences of getting caught would be phoning a probation officer periodically or picking up litter one or two Saturdays why not risk committing the crime? The benefits far outweigh the risks.

Even with harsher sentences being handed out some crime rates would remain the same. Crimes of passion and crimes related to drugs would probably occur at their previous rates. Crimes committed by career criminals may also remain unchanged. However, there would still be a significant impact on the crimes being committed by people who just aren't worried about getting caught. These people would definitely think twice before embarking on a crime spree if they were certain that getting caught would lead to a sentence they were not willing to accept.

Something is wrong when so many people—especially juveniles—are joking and celebrating after returning from their court appearances. They "moved" the judge to give them another chance and then laugh at the judge and the system all the way to their next offense. On the way they make sure they tell their friends how easy it all was. Judges need to get out of their courtrooms more.

The legal system today is about prosecutors, judges and clerks who are so mired in paperwork, delays, gamesmanship, procedures, deals, and sheer volume that "justice" has slipped far down the list of priorities. "Justice" today is more about saving time and finding shortcuts.

Many Americans also feel that the legal system has deteriorated to the point that criminals love it and law abiding citizens dread it. To repeat offenders, going to court poses no threat. It's nothing more than an inconvenience. Cases are thrown out everyday on technicalities, most of which are ridiculous. Suspended or light sentences are laughed at by the criminals and their lawyers. Tough sentences, when they actually do occur, are appealed and at times overturned. During a trial, the victim, the police department, the lab and any other entity involved in trying to prosecute the offender are fair game and are often attacked and even intimidated by the "defense attorney."

I don't know about you, but I have long since lost respect for anything legal. When it comes to dealing with courts and lawyers, I would prefer to be the criminal. Is it any wonder police departments are overworked and burnt out? Is there any excuse, any excuse at all, that criminals with a 10 page long "rap sheet" are out on the streets committing other crimes?

How many more times will we hear about a violent, heartbreaking crime, locally or nationally, that was committed by an offender with a long history of crime? Why is it so difficult to impose sentences on these people that will get them off the streets after their first or second crime?

Isn't it ridiculous that we are letting ourselves be victimized on a regular basis by criminals who were not effectively dealt with by our judges in the first place? How any judge can show his/her face in public knowing they are considered allies by the criminals and incompetent by the very people they are suppose to be protecting is beyond me.

When rating lawyers, and now judges too, on the list of most respected people, Americans consistently rank them at or near the bottom of the list. It's incredible that the very people who claim they are the defenders of the law, the dispute settlers, the seekers of justice are virtual outcasts in our society when it comes to public opinion. Lawyers rank about as high in respect as tax collectors did in biblical times. Yet nothing changes. Lawyer jokes abound.

Most Americans consider lawyers to be dishonest, fast-talking, money grabbing shysters who couldn't care less about the law. They are only in the "business" to make money and to make a name for themselves. (I have to let prosecutors off the hook on this one. They have a tough job and aren't paid nearly as well). What does this tell us about our legal system? In a perfect world, with perfect lawyers, they would be at the top of the list of most revered professionals.

I believe a major contributing factor to the state our legal system is indeed the judges. There are few "judgeships" which are available to persons who are not lawyers. These are the positions in small rural towns. The remaining categories require that the person becoming a judge must first have been a lawyer. That makes sense on paper, but one side effect is that it makes the legal system a close-knit little community—a fraternity if you will. A lawyer works side by side with the people in the system until one day he/she becomes a judge. Supposedly the bonds they formed as attorneys don't influence their decisions on the bench. In addition, it means the pool from which judges come is one in which all of its members have been subjected to the same educational and procedural influences. It's basically a culture unto itself. Most judges are the same because most lawyers are the same. There just isn't enough "outside" influence to shake things up. Consequently, the legal system has become stagnant. It is a product of "in-breeding."

Here is another factor which I believe is negatively affecting our legal system. Once a judge almost always a judge. By that I mean that judges know once they make it to the bench it is very difficult for the public to get rid of them. Even though most are elected and their actions can be subjected to a judiciary review board, it is rare that judges ever lose their positions. It is very difficult for the public to keep track of a judge's record. There are no statistics or other data, readily available, that would help the public rate a sitting judge. Unless a judge's rulings make the news they conduct their courtrooms with little public scrutiny.

Any police officer could tell you the names of the judges who consistently dole out light sentences, or throw cases out. We all know that there are such judges. However, it is not in the officer's best interest to name names because that officer will find himself/herself in front of those judges during the normal course of their workday. Would you tell the public how incompetent your boss was in hopes that your boss would step down or be fired knowing that if you failed you would still have to work for him/her everyday afterward?

Here's an idea. Why don't we just vote against any judge seeking re-election unless they have stood out during their term as being a hard-nosed judge? What have we got to lose? The system isn't working now anyway. That means no judge would stay in their position for more than four years (except federal judges). I think the public should make it a point to vote whenever judges are on the ballot. Forget about all the other candidates if you must. Concentrate on the judges. They have more impact on your life. Unless the sitting judge has earned a reputation via the media, word of mouth, and perhaps statistically (which would be difficult to do) vote for the person running against that judge. It wouldn't be long before judges would focus more on the public they are suppose to be protecting instead of the criminals they get to know.

So think about it. Let's make judges understand that once they are elected we are giving them four years to impress us. If they do not—see ya!

What about attorneys? I know this sounds crazy, but I think any lawyer who helps an offender go free because of a technicality, legal maneuvering or overpowering an overworked and underpaid prosecutor should be considered an "accessory" to any future crime committed by that offender. Why shouldn't they be? Isn't that the same as though they took the keys, unlocked the cell and let the criminal out?

These lawyers are not the "protectors of liberty and justice" as they so often proclaim. They are not protecting us from injustice. They are perpetrating injustice. Justice may be blind, but it doesn't have to be stupid.

Spare me the rhetoric about not understanding the system or about how it's more complicated than what I am saying. I don't want to hear about how my freedom and rights are being protected by all the shenanigans that go on in a court room. At this point, I would rather take my chances on being falsely accused in a safer world, than remain a potential target in a more dangerous world in which my rights are supposedly so well protected!

Here are just two tragic examples of how our "system" is failing:

In 2003 a teenage boy is sentenced to 33 years in prison for repeatedly raping a four year old family member. Incredibly he ended up being given 5 years probation—for raping a four year old child! The judge and other "professionals" felt that he was a good candidate for therapy and rehabilitation. No jail time would be needed.

Shortly thereafter this criminal was hired to work at a theater frequented by young people. One night he raped and then murdered a 16 yr. old high school student in the theater. He later stuffed her body in a storage area and concealed it with a vending machine. Nice call judge.

Recently, we experienced the tragedy involving 11 year old Carlie Bruscia. We all saw the video replay of her being escorted to her death by a man on probation. How chilling is that? We saw the images of her last human encounter. We watched the video knowing that her life was about to be snuffed out by the very person who was leading her away.

When I think of the heartache I would experience if that had been one of my daughters I quickly erase the image. It's just too horrific, too devastating. What makes this crime even more tragic is that the predator who killed this innocent child was roaming freely because a judge ruled not to revoke his probation in spite of being asked to do so by the probation officer. Another nice call.

Why should any child have to experience what Carlie experienced? It's horrific to think that what she suffered was at the hands of a "repeat offender" who but for some "technicality" should have been in jail.

These two cases are not exceptions. As I am sure you would agree, such lapses in judgment occur every single day. They are becoming routine. It's the current mentality of our judges—so many are trying to "save" the offenders.

"Let's see. The crime has already been committed. The victim and the victim's family are already suffering. I know! I will see what I can do to help the offender!" They pass out sentences all day, every day, to the point they become jaded and careless. Yet another reason we should vote for new judges every four years.

I have often wondered what percentage of crime in America is being committed by repeat offenders who were on probation, or had received light sentences for earlier crimes. How many other crimes are being committed by people who just weren't afraid of the "consequences" they saw other offenders getting?

Judges and other "professionals" who are entrusted to protect innocent people need to be held more accountable when they do a sloppy, careless job. Look at how other professionals are treated who have the safety of other people in their hands. If a pilot missed the runway and landed in a mall parking lot—even if nobody died—the pilot would face disciplinary action. If the plane careened into a crowd of people there is no doubt he would never fly commercially again. People are dying everyday because lawyers and judges keep releasing criminals who go out and re-offend.

When judges screw up they should do some community service. Perhaps serving the families victimized by the criminals they let off the hook would be fair and reasonable. They owe these families at least that much.

The Ten Commandments
(Revised)

Here are the revised "ten" commandments. You will notice that all references to God (except one) have been removed in order to not to offend anyone. They have been modified to accommodate as many popular ways of thinking as possible. If the Ten Commandments were more user-friendly, more flexible, then perhaps more people would abide by them. They are listed in no particular order so as to avoid implying one was more important than another. See what you think.

Thou shalt not steal Unless you think you won't get caught. Or steal a little at a time so if you do get caught there won't be any consequences. Besides no one misses little quantities of anything.

Thou shalt not take the Lord's name in vain. Don't even worry about this one. You are protected by the First Amendment.

Thou shalt not kill unless you have an attorney who will blame it on your parents and teachers, and then get you released because of a "bungled" police investigation.

Thou shalt not covet thy neighbor's wife unless she also covets you. Perhaps a swap would be possible or maybe a threesome. If you're lucky maybe you could get the two wives together!

Honor thy father and thy mother unless they are insisting that you do things you don't feel like doing. For example if they are expecting you to be responsible, apply yourself at school and in life, obey all laws, and respect others. Remember if things get really bad you can file a complaint against them. Judges will throw the book at 'em. There are plenty left from all the ones they didn't throw at the real criminals.

Thou shalt not covet thy neighbor's goods unless they have something you really want. Wait for them to leave it out and then take it.

Thou shalt not bear false witness against thy neighbor unless you are expecting them to settle out of court. That way nobody gets hurt and you make a little cash. It's a win-win situation.

Thou shalt not commit adultery unless you are sure your partner won't find out. After all no one is getting hurt.

Keep holy the Sabbath unless there is a really good game on or if you have had a tough week and need the extra rest. Worship can be so inconvenient some times. When in doubt turn to a religious program for a few minutes during a commercial break in the game.

Thou shalt remember that an act is only wrong if you get caught so for godsake be careful!

Good vs. Evil

Goodness for the most part is a constant. Good people can only be so good. They can only be so generous, so loving, so honest, etc. Goodness can't evolve more than it already was when it began. The number of good people can grow, but individually once a person is "good" all they can then do is try to maintain their "goodness". By that I mean that a good person by constantly being good will not one day acquire some special power over evil. Being good is as powerful as good ever gets. In a free society, while goodness remains unchanged, evil keeps redefining itself.

This is too important to ignore. Good people have always been locked in a struggle with evil people. There seems to be an ebb and flow to this battle. Tragically, the odds are against that which is good. By that I mean it's just easier to be evil. It's easier to destroy than it is to build. It's easier to lash out than it is to hold back. In a group and especially in a society it takes fewer people to sabotage or destroy collective harmony than it does to achieve it. Anyone can be a "destroyer". Try being a "builder".

Look at our daily lives today. One person can intimidate a community. A handful of people can wreck havoc on a country. A larger group can terrorize the world. When good prevails in an individual, group or country it must do so against all odds.

Even though there has been evil and suffering in every generation, is this a time when evil, in all of its forms, is overtaking that which is good? Look at the evil we live with today. It continues to permeate all parts of our lives. It grows virtually unchecked—and in some cases—with the assistance of the very people it is destroying.

Whenever there are weak boundaries, or worse, no boundaries at all, goodness and those who embrace it will have to endure stronger and stronger attacks from evil and those who embrace it. There is nothing to stop them.

Disagree with me if you must. But no one can deny the direction our society is heading. Can any basically good human being, actually say with conviction that they don't feel threatened today? Do they not worry about their children on a daily basis? Are children safer and more moral than they once were? Is our country more peaceful and harmonious than it's ever been before?

Most good people struggle silently everyday trying to escape the clutches of evil. In doing so, they tend to be less involved and less passionate because they fear doing otherwise might draw evil's attention toward them. They have built little fortresses of security in their lives hoping that evil will not find them. However, evil does find some of them each and every day. Like a cold-hearted monster with an icy stare it swoops down upon the innocent and snatches them away from the delicate peace which once embraced them.

How many beautiful, loving, innocent people were kidnapped, raped, abused, tortured or murdered recently? Are crimes not becoming more horrific and more numerous? When people speak up about such things they are always met with loud, relentless resistance by those who will be threatened by such attacks. Good people fight "by the rules". Evil people have no rules. It's just not a fair fight. Therefore evil left unchecked, or ignored, or overlooked will eventually overtake whatever target it sets its eyes on—including an entire society.

Are we Americans as "good" as we can be? Are we becoming more evil than those who lived one or two generations ago?

I am not saying today's Americans are more evil than any humans since the beginning of time. We all know that there were tremendous atrocities being perpetrated by humans against other humans throughout history. Man's inhumanity to man is well documented and seems timeless.

However, was there a time when things were actually better? Did they pass us by? Is it possible that our society escaped the clutches of rampant evil, progressed to a point when people were safer and more at peace and then began to slide back into the powerful clutches of unrestrained evil where we now find ourselves?

Are we doomed to experience the same kinds of torture, murder, abuses, atrocities and perversions that were rampant hundreds, or even thousands of years ago? Why after thousands of years have we still not found peace and harmony? Does it take four thousand years? Seven thousand years? Or does the fact we are still struggling, trying to overcome the same destructive forces as those who lived generations ago mean that good will never prevail?

I understand that there will always be a struggle between good and evil. I am just wondering which side has fought the better battle.

Carter vs. Clinton

Am I the only person who wondered what former President Jimmy Carter thinks of the Bill Clinton/Monica Lewinsky scandal?

Do you remember how the country reacted about 22 years earlier when Jimmy Carter, the then Democratic candidate for the presidency, uttered his famous "lusting" remark in the November 1976 Playboy interview?

> *"I've looked on a lot of women with lust. I've committed adultery in my heart many times. This is something that God recognizes I will do—and I have done it—and God forgives me for it."*

Here was a man, running for president, making an honest admission that he had thoughts of adultery. That's right, he said he had "thoughts" about adultery. He was telling us the truth about some of his thoughts right in the middle of his campaign. I repeat—he was being truthful.

After the interview was released, Mr. Carter had to endure a firestorm of public criticism and ridicule. People were outraged about such an admission. He was the punchline to many jokes. It could have easily been even worse. However, the country was still reeling from the lengthy, emotionally draining Watergate scandal and the subsequent resignation of President Richard Nixon.

It was thought that this honest statement could have very easily caused Mr. Carter the election—which it didn't. Many people believe that the country was so unforgiving of Richard Nixon that they voted against Gerald Ford for pardoning him. Consequently, in spite of the furor that erupted over Jimmy Carter's "lusting", he did go on to win the election.

As for Bill Clinton, it's true he weathered an emotional controversy similar to that which was experienced by Jimmy Carter. However while many Americans said Jimmy Carter's name with indignation and contempt, they speak Bill Clinton's name with a wink and a jab.

Bill Clinton is most remembered for saying, "I did not have sexual relations with that woman, Monica Lewinsky." Unlike Carter, Clinton was not telling the truth. In fact he was lying to the entire country, while looking with sincerity and confidence into the camera. Unlike Carter, Clinton did more than just *think* about adultery.

Of course Mr. Clinton was impeached by the House of Representatives for the crimes of perjury to a federal grand jury and obstruction of justice. He was also disbarred, stripped of his license to practice law and found in contempt of court by an Arkansas federal judge. He was fined $90,686 for giving false testimony in a law suit filed against him by Paula Jones. In addition he paid an out of court settlement to Paula Jones of $850,000.

In spite of all that, Clinton remains very popular with many Americans. So much so, Mr. Clinton is paid tens of thousands of dollars a night for speaking engagements. He is still considered to be a major player in the Democratic party.

So I wonder what Jimmy Carter would say he felt in his heart while seeing Bill Clinton continue to gain favor with so many Americans after doing something that Carter was blasted for merely thinking about. In the span of only 22 years could things have changed that much?

I also wonder at times if Mr. Clinton had been treated more appropriately by Congress, or if he had conducted himself differently as the President of the United States, would there have been a more positive effect in the classrooms and homes in America?

No one can be sure what impact, if any, Clinton's behavior may have had on our youth. However, I have seen numerous examples in the behaviors of students who followed his lead. Two examples of the negative effect his conduct has had on our children were mentioned on national television.

One was a guest on *Oprah*. One of Oprah's guests was a lady who is a specialist dealing with young teens and preteens who are already engaging in sexual activity. She cited Mr. Clinton's definition of "sex" as one that is being embraced by an alarming number of children today. That is, oral sex really isn't sex at all. Consequently kids, as early as in middle school, are engaging in oral sex (mostly girls on guys) and not thinking anything of it.

The other reference was made during a *Primetime* telecast on ABC. It was an hour long program on the dramatic rise in cheating by students across America. When asked if they thought cheating was wrong, students made reference to the Enron scandal, lawyers routinely getting guilty people "off" and Bill Clinton—while in the highest office in the land—lying about his relationship with Monica Lewinsky, as indications why they no longer worried about their own cheating.

Here is something else to consider. When I was growing up I would often hear references to "becoming President of the United States" being made by adults and children as one of the great aspirations one could have. It was also mentioned as something extraordinary any honorable American might one day achieve. Do parents still brag about their children by saying, "One day he/she will become the President!"? Why is becoming the president of the United States no longer routinely mentioned as an honorable, dignified aspiration?

I am not suggesting that Bill Clinton is responsible for all the ills in our society. These are just thoughts I've had. I wonder if Jimmy Carter or you have had them too.

Impure Politics

Democracy is awesome. I am grateful that I was born in America where democracy rules. I cannot imagine living under any other form of government. The best thing about a democracy is that we get to choose our leaders and other government officials. We can either vote them in or vote them out during our elections. Elections require candidates. Candidates usually have some party affiliation. Unfortunately candidates and their parties also have a "political" agenda. There's the rub. Politics spawns politicians. The downside to our democracy is that we have to endure politicians.

Am I the only American who feels frustrated and even insulted whenever political candidates, or their spokespeople, open their mouths? Surely I am not alone in noticing that rarely do any of these people ever say anything original or meaningful. Rather they proceed to spout off some litany of prepared gibberish intent only on attacking their most threatening opponent.

Why do they think it's acceptable—and that we don't notice—for them to avoid a question or in some cases change the question? Why do they use the opportunity to answer a question as a way to say whatever they think will serve them better? They do this even if their response has nothing to do with what was asked. I find this "accepted" practice highly irritating. One would think that politicians would eventually grow tired of being near the bottom of the "most trusted and respected" list and start to change their ways.

What's even worse, totally intolerable to me, are the "mouthpieces" for the parties and/or the candidates. These pontificating, narrow-minded, "spokespeople" are becoming more and more abusive and insulting. They remind me of professional wrestlers challenging each other to their next match. Professional wrestlers however are more creative, much more entertaining and have acknowledged that they are just putting on a show.

The political mouthpieces are spewing their one-sided spittle as though it were the only truth. They do so with such arrogance I personally find them offensive.

Regardless of the facts, the mouthpieces and candidates go on and on about all the ills in society that the opposing party has created. When confronted by an interviewer with facts or figures which don't support the candidate's position they immediately ignore the facts, distort them, or change the subject.

For example if an interviewer states information that seem to weaken the candidate's or spokesperson's position they will respond with something like, "Well that may be, but do the American people really want a president (for example) who voted against the crime bill? Do Americans want a leader who is weak on defense?"

When candidates or their spokesfolks appear on talk shows with an opponent, or their representative, it has become routine to see them constantly interrupt not only each other but also the host. Going back to professional wrestlers, you will rarely, if ever, see them interrupt each other during their verbal exchanges. Not so with politicians. Their behavior is nothing short of unprofessional and embarrassing. They could learn from professional wrestlers.

Here is a thought I hope you have had too. I wish politicians would stop insulting me. Please, stop insulting my intelligence. While you are at it, stop insulting your opponent and the other party every time you speak. Do us all a favor and learn some courtesy and respect. You need to know that no matter how important you feel you are, or how "right" you think you are, there are many of us who have long since stopped laughing at your ridiculous behavior. We now just turn our heads in disgust. You are an embarrassment.

How do you expect us to respect you when you never show respect to your opponent or to us? It seems you are unable to ever acknowledge that the opposing party or the opposing candidate might have some good ideas. No matter what is stated, if it was stated by the opposing party, you claim it's wrong.

(As a side note, what about the ridiculous display of partisan immaturity in congress when the president is giving a speech? Am I the only one who is tired of seeing members from the other party sitting with their arms crossed across their chests with bored disinterested faces, refusing to applaud? I actually look forward to the camera panning these "public servants" so I can laugh as I see them acting like spoiled children. These are our top "leaders").

As for presidential campaign promises let us not forget that a president cannot cut taxes, increase jobs, or pass any legislation. They can only influence the American public, "work" the members of Congress, set the tone and veto legislation.

It's time for presidential candidates to stop telling us all the changes they are going to make. Congress can make the changes. The president can only suggest them. In the future, let's all remember to give Congress the credit for the things we are happy with and the blame for the things which disappointed us. If you are unhappy with taxes, jobs, health care and the like, forget the presidential candidates, concentrate on the congressional candidates.

Politicians often refer to themselves as "public servants". They present themselves as people who care about us. They tell us they chose "public service" as a way to "make a difference". Am I the only person who sees that in reality their first priority is actually getting and staying elected?

I am tired of nationally known politicians referring to themselves as "public servants." I have a message for them. When you lower your salaries to $40,000 or less, get rid of the limos, the perks, the offices, the freebies and discounts and start to live like a teacher, police officer, fireman, sanitation worker, and such then you may call yourself a "public servant."

I want to see politicians in America set higher standards and live by them. I want to see candidates run "for" something instead of "against" someone. Candidates should simply tell us specifically what they stand for and what they intend to do if elected. They should also listen to other candidates and be willing to acknowledge better ideas when they hear them.

Wouldn't it be refreshing, as well as inspiring, to hear a candidate say about an opponent's idea, "Wow, that is a great idea. If I am elected I would like to incorporate that into my programs as well—with your permission of course."

Let's face it, far too many candidates merely employ a "strategy" that they believe will help them win the election. They are not telling us what they think. Instead they are telling us what they think we want to hear. Elections should not be about winning at all costs for one party or another.

Campaigns should be a forum of idea presenting. Those running for office should present their ideas and then wait to see how the voters vote. Candidates should stop wasting our time by constantly discrediting their opponents and the opponents' ideas. Candidates should prefer losing an election honestly than winning it by name calling, misinformation and employing a "better strategy".

Finally, it seems to me that most people wanting fame, fortune and power often choose a career in the fields of entertainment, the media or professional sports. Those who lack the patience, persistence and/or talent to do that often choose politics. To paraphrase an adage which is regrettably all too true, the people best suited for public office would never run. Who does that leave?

This Just In

I have much to say about nationally televised news. Pull up a chair.

There is no doubt that the news media can be a wonderful resource for information while also serving as a deterrent to or "exposer" of corruption. There are ways in which the media can help improve and even protect us.

However, just like every other entity the media is prone to mistakes, misjudgments and irresponsibly. The problem is that the media is seldom held accountable for its lapses.

It seems to me that the national news media has too much power, too much influence, and too much room to operate. It's not their fault. We let them. They have created an image that lulls us into thinking that the media is made up of righteous people who are dedicated to providing us with a service we couldn't live without.

They portray themselves as determined watch dogs sniffing out evil, and as "professional" information gatherers scouring the landscape to keep the rest of us up to date on the latest happenings.

In truth, the media nothing more than a large group people, just like you and me, going out each day to earn a living.

The media has built a "net-work" around us which in essence filters all information in and out. They decide what events are important and which ones are not. They routinely imply who is good and insinuate who is bad. Without ever admitting it, the news media routinely "passes judgment" on the people and events they are covering, all the while presenting what they insist is their unbiased reporting on each.

One of the most disappointing aspects of the news media is all too often they are nothing more than "tattletales". In many other situations they act like hunters and treat all others as the hunted.

As a rule, the media can't wait to show some person's mistake or misfortune. The majority of these blunders can hardly be considered news, but we see them virtually everyday.

Whether it is a celebrity's faux paus, a politician's misstatement, or someone's brush with the law, the camera crews will rush to get the "story."

Whenever people fall on their faces, there's a good chance it will be captured and covered by the news media. This practice has made the media nothing more than "mistake vultures." They spend each day circling the skies waiting to capitalize on someone else's misfortune.

As soon as some poor soul trips and falls, the mistake vultures swoop down to get their feed. It's interesting that one standard technical term used in broadcasting is the term "feed". For example, "This is a live *feed* from just outside the courthouse." Well at least they chose an appropriate term.

In addition, they "tattle" on people whose actions, although illegal or at the very least inappropriate will result in the embarrassment of an entire institution or even our country.

Their rush to be the first to get the story, at all costs, has proven costly indeed. It's a times like these—when the media is doing nothing more than tattling—that they get the rest of the class in trouble too.

At the same time we are constantly bombarded with imagery chosen by the media to enhance our perception of those delivering the news. This "game" is played by their rules.

We will never see a camera crew barging in on a news anchor before every hair is in place, each wrinkle covered and all buttons buttoned. We won't see any reports on those in the media exposing their own tax fraud, DUIs, "indiscretions", or the other missteps and miscues they so often report when committed by others.

Do you think we will ever see an "investigative report" by ABC news offering a "behind the scenes look at inappropriate dealings" engaged in by CBS who was in the process of a "hidden camera" investigation exposing false statements and cover ups by NBC who was preparing an undercover report on the questionable practices of ABC?

What do you think would happen if a "renegade" group of reporters started delving into the personal lives and professional practices of every person in the media? What would happen if those in the media were subjected to the same scrutiny as they themselves impose on others?

This is what we see instead. Each news show is preceded by musical "fanfare" beating out a "tickertape" like rhythm throbbing with a sense of urgency. Bold, important-looking graphics fill the screen announcing the beginning of yet another presentation of the dramatic occurrences of the day.

We are shown lavish sets and perfectly groomed news anchors. Those "in the field" are shown as hard-working professionals. Perhaps their sleeves are rolled up or their hair slightly out of place as they give us the most up to date information from the scene. "No time for wardrobe and makeup I gotta get the story."

There is one important truth that is never acknowledged by those in televised news. After you clear away the smoke and clean all of the mirrors what you will see is the true driving force reigning over every news department—ratings.

News programs have stated that they ignore ratings, but their actions speak louder than their words. If ratings aren't important why do news departments spend so much time and money on self-promotion?

Does a day go by when we don't hear a news program proudly proclaiming "You saw it here first." Or "We're the most watched." They tell us how their's is the station that gives us "news you can trust." Or "We are your number one source for news." Their reporting routinely includes phrases like, "seen only on" and "This is exclusive video".

Commercials for every news station include their ratings performance and reasons why they are better than the competition. Do we need to be reminded constantly that we aren't just getting news, we are getting "award winning" news?

If news programs weren't concerned with ratings why have they resorted to the use of "teases"? For example, "Can eating certain kinds of seafood kill you? We'll give you the answer tonight at ten." "Do you shop at a so-called discount store? You won't believe what we found. You won't want to miss this shocking story Thursday night at 5:00."

Isn't that just a little too obvious? Are the news departments embarrassed at all by the use of such ploys?

What if the average person resorted to such antics?

"Guess what? Did you know that there is a way that you could die from drinking that? I'll tell you how tomorrow night at 10:00."

"Hey dude, did you know that I am the number one, best, most requested, award-winningest employee in this entire company? You should follow me around so I can tell you more about why I am better than everyone else." "Be sure to get here tomorrow at 5:00 so you can watch me in action."

There is so much self-promotion and image-creating it's easy to forget that those in the televised news business are just people like the rest of us. They are no more dedicated or honest or important than the people they are covering.

They haven't been "called" to some higher vocation. They aren't sacrificing or risking any more than millions of other Americans in less glamorous, more scrutinized professions.

Here is something I find interesting. No matter what has happened in the world on any given day, reporting it always takes 30 minutes-no more-no less. So that which is considered news must be relative.

What might be news on one day may not be news the next. It all depends on what else happened. Wouldn't it be more appropriate if on some days the newscasters finished reading their teleprompters in perhaps16 minutes? Then simply say, "Well that's all the news we have for you today."

Whenever a news department feels an event is particularly traumatic or important they will air "special reports" that pre-empt regularly scheduled programming. News people love those opportunities.

Have you ever noticed the restrained excitement in the reporter's face and hear the controlled enthusiasm in his/her voice when there is a breaking story? Of course they are trying to act aloof and professional. But let's face it, for them it's an exciting day at work.

Whether it is a natural catastrophe, an act of terrorism or some equally traumatic situation, the whole news department struggles to contain their excitement. This is a chance for them to become part of the story, part of history. This is when the ol' adrenalin gets pumping. Whenever there is breaking news a reporter can't wait to get to work.

The media also tends to "favor" stories they feel will attract the most viewers. They will pass on the not so "glamorous" yet important stories to cover the ones which will be more exciting.

It's dramatic and sensational to cover natural disasters like tornados, hurricanes and fires. It's compelling to list the number of American soldiers who died on any given day in an ongoing war. It's titillating to be outside of the courtroom during the trial of a well-known celebrity or public figure. It's attention-getting to show video of a ship sinking in an ocean halfway around the world.

How important or relevant are many of these stories when compared to more traumatic, but less interesting events?

Imagine the changes which might occur if the media chose to deal with the not so glamorous issues and reported them on a daily basis. Do you think it would make a difference if we were told the number of children and teens who died or were killed each day right here in America?

If we were reminded everyday of the "body count" which resulted from suicides, drug overdoses, homicides, alcohol-related deaths, kidnappings and rapes involving our children would the resulting public outcry help prevent some of these tragedies in the future?

These losses greatly outnumber the casualties of war. Why are they ignored? Why does the news media not consider them newsworthy?

These losses may not be as "honorable" as those in a war, but they are just as real and have considerably more impact on us.

I fully understand why the loss of every American soldier is "newsworthy". I am by no means minimizing their sacrifice or their significance. Not a day goes by that I don't bow my head and pray out of concern and respect for every soldier—living and dead.

I just don't understand why the media isn't interested in all of the other innocent lives which are tragically ended each and everyday in our own streets and cities. Once again, the media is deciding what is "newsworthy" and what isn't.

Whenever the media is covering an on-going story, their coverage can also affect public opinion in a negative way. The media takes it upon themselves to expose actions and behaviors before all the facts are known. This leads to misrepresentations and misinformation that dramatically impacts those involved in an unfair way.

The media is not just an innocent bystander the way they like to portray themselves. In truth, they are manipulating the very events they are covering. They become part of the event. By doing so, in many situations, the media even affects the final outcome. Examples of this would include elections, trials, trends and policy-making.

The media is wielding its power, shaping events and our reactions to those events all the while acting like objective observers who are just doing their jobs.

There are other forms of "slanting" a story we can see everyday. For example, let's say a network is doing a story about a popular president.

The vast majority of the time you will see a photo or video showing him well groomed, smiling, interacting with others, or waving to the crowd. You've seen it as often as I have.

However, if it is a story about an unpopular president—or a president they want to make unpopular—we will be shown a frowning, disheveled president. He will be shown rushing into his limo, or quickly entering a building or office.

Simply by choosing the visual which accompanies the story, the sequence in which the story is edited and the words used in the story, the reporter/editor creates a particular reaction or feeling to the story.

I maintain that whatever reaction we have to a story is the very reaction the media wants us to have. To pretend or deny this isn't true and doesn't happen every single day is ridiculous.

Consider that same story accompanied by even more favorable images of the president. For example, using images of the president playing with his dog, giving his kids piggyback rides, or serving food to the homeless. Do you think that story might evoke yet a different reaction?

Here is another form of slanting. The reporter ends the story with a tag line containing innuendo or subtle opinion. For example,

"The President will be flying later today to Camp David to meet with his top advisors. They will be discussing what options are available to handle this critical situation. *Whether they will be able to stem the tide of an already angry public remains to be seen. Richard Mediaman XYZ News, Washington*".

What was the purpose of the final sentence? Was it part of the reporting of Who? What? When? Where? Why? Does adding a tag line like that slant the story? Would I have felt differently about the situation and the people involved if I had simply been informed that the president and his top advisors were meeting and that it would be this weekend, at Camp David, to discuss options?

What about an opposite "slant"?

"The President will be flying later today to Camp David to meet with his top advisors. They will be discussing what options are available to handle this critical situation. *The President and his staff will undoubtedly rise to the occasion once again and put to rest the concerns of an angry public.*"

I feel much better about that situation. Don't you?

Another example of slanting, again using the President of the United States, is ignoring the proper title of "President." I find it highly disrespectful, in poor taste and a form of slanting whenever newscasters, or others in the media, refer to the current President by name.

Using the president who was in office as this book was being written as an example, the reporter will say, "Mr. Bush" or "George Bush" instead of using his professional title, "President Bush".

It makes no difference to me to which party a president belongs. The President of the United States should be referred to as such. It seems the less a newscaster or reporter likes a particular person, the less willing they are to use their professional title. It's their way of letting you know they don't like the man.

To show you just how far the arrogance of the media extends allow me to ask you this,

"Is there anything more insulting and meaningless than listening to newscasters or 'political experts' tell us what the President just said after giving a speech?"

Why do newscasters think that we didn't understand it ourselves? Is the implication that they have some special intelligence or insight that we don't have? I hope I am not the only person who changes the channel to something else as soon as the speech is completed.

I really want these "political experts" and anchors to know that as they are telling me again, what I had just listened to, I am no longer listening. You might as well be talking to each other in the hallway.

Let's face it. A large percentage of the stories reported to us each and every day/night are events that we really can't do anything about and will have no real impact on our daily lives. News programs are simply finding the most interesting, most graphic, and most titillating stories they can to fill their time slot that day.

It seems relatively insignificant stories, comparatively speaking, take on even more importance if the network has video of the event. Consequently, a story that might not have otherwise made the broadcast will certainly be included if there is "dramatic" video.

It seems to me that is just another example of what networks considers "news" is rather arbitrary. The news media may tell us differently, but they are in denial if they really believe they are always reporting real "news".

It is even more distressing when there is "breaking news" the way the anchor and field reporters attempt to keep our attention by exaggerating the "drama". Then they insist on telling us the same facts over and over, with little variation, while they await some exciting update. Surely their favorite phrase has to be, "This just in."

To make matters worse, they act like we don't realize they are repeating themselves. They use a different camera angle or mix up the sentences a little implying that we must be sitting at home thinking, "Wow, that was even more interesting than the first five times you told me that." Please, when there is nothing going on, stop pretending that there is. You are not fooling anyone.

Here is this most serious question of all. How many events in the modern past occurred as a direct result of a person or persons wanting to become instant celebrities knowing that the media would rush to cover "the story"? Consequently, how many tragic events have we endured that were actually spawned by the media's potential coverage?

I think that the conclusion is inescapable. Some of the most sensational news stories and the victims they left in their wake were the direct result of one or more people wanting to get attention from the media, which of course they did.

Does that make the media somewhat responsible for those past events and for the ones awaiting us in the future?

Trends

I have always been fascinated by trends. What is it that first sparks a trend and then causes so many people to jump on the bandwagon? All trends are known to be just that—a trend. They are simply temporary events or behaviors. Yet numerous people rush to be participants. Since fads and trends are so important in America I thought I would give you my perspective on them.

There are basically four groups involved in trends.

The first group is comprised of those folks who actually originate the trend. That could mean that they conceived of it, or that they borrowed it from a previous generation and either modified it or claimed it as it was. In the world of trends, these folks at least had some initiative and originality. They are the creators, the originators.

The next group consists of those who simply follow a trend. Why? I suppose for a sense of belonging. Also, following a trend is a way for one to express one's "individuality". It's a form of expression that people use to make a statement about themselves.

Trends are considered new and what is happening. They're cool so anyone participating must be cool too. Trends are thought to distinguish one generation from another. Basically I understand all of this.

However, when you break this group down into its simplest form the conclusion is that the people in this group are primarily followers, with little or no imagination of their own. They are nothing more than "copycats".

If you are a man from the same generation as me, you no doubt have pictures from your past of yourself with long hair, probably parted in the middle and dangling down to your shoulders. Were you dressed in a paisley shirt and bell bottoms? Surely our generation has the most embarrassing wedding pictures of any generation. We were nothing more than trend followers. Embarrassing isn't it?

Similarly, if you have your tongue, lip, nose, eyebrow, belly button or any other part of your body pierced, or have a barbed wire tattoo around one or both of your arms, or a tattoo on your lower back, then you are a trend follower too. You too will one day look at pictures of yourself and wonder what you were thinking.

The third group consists of those who have to take a fad or trend to its extreme. This is most easily seen with something like tattoos, piercings, hair, etc. For tattoos, obviously this is the person who gets his/her entire body covered. Then there is always someone who takes that to an extreme and covers his/her face as well. It's a form of "one upsmanship. "Look at me. Look how original, creative and bold I am".

Also in this category are those who seek to "push the boundaries" as though they are explorers willing to be the ones who shape our morals and influence the direction our society may be taking. They present themselves as artists, risk-takers, rebels or as necessary influences who make us "look at ourselves".

These are the people who think boundaries are there to be broken. What a lame excuse for malcontents and ego-based people to get attention. Look at the trends in this category. For example, in the world of music/entertainment we went from being shaken up by the "long" hair and bangs sported by the Beatles to the antics and appearance of Marilyn Manson or Rob Zombie. Some people even identify with or admire these "risk-takers."

Surely I am not the only person who knows that being provocative or shocking is the easiest way to get attention. Anyone with or without talent, with or without skill, and with or without basic intelligence can choose to dress or act bizarrely. Please, for those of you about to attempt to shock us by your unorthodox behavior, spare us the boredom. Shock us by your kindness, respect and generosity. That would be revolutionary!

The fourth group consists of those who are unable or unwilling to participate in a trend. Just because the fad or trend is considered to be the newest "craze" is not enough reason for these folks to get on board.

Interestingly enough, as trends become embraced by more and more people, it is those who did not "succumb" to the fad who, by their non-participation, begin to emerge as the trendsetters. For example, so many teenagers have tattoos now that those who have chosen not to get one are becoming the new trendsetters.

Fads begin to die out when the older generation begins to embrace them. It's humorous to me when fads or trends become embraced by the very people who were the "targets" of the original movement. These people were not intended to be participants.

For example, when the trend for males to start sporting pierced ears gained favor not so long ago it began in younger men. It was meant to be fashionable and "hip". This included musicians, artists and athletes. The next thing you know pierced ears started to appear on older men. I suppose it is an attempt to be fashionable or "hip." Harrison Ford, the actor and Ed Bradley of *60 Minutes,* are just two examples. I smiled when I saw them with their little ear piercings.

Now you can find pierced ears on businessmen, doctors, teachers and others. These are hardly the people for whom the trend was originally intended. I think that's funny. Come to think of it, I still haven't seen pierced ears on any presidential candidates. That would really end the trend!

"Leave me a canteen and a rifle...."

I have a short observation about heroism I would like to share with you.

When I was growing up I was surrounded by real and imaginary men and women who possessed honor, bravery and dignity. I saw them in real life. I saw them on television. I saw them at the movies. It seemed that I was surrounded by heroic people and their stories.

There were examples of great men and women shown to us in war, politics, sports, law enforcement, and virtually every other area of life. In the movies it might be a soldier, a cowboy, a policeman or fireman. Perhaps it was a movie about a priest or nun, or a generous business man.

My friends and I were inundated with stories, real and imagined, of heroes. When we played we pretended we were heroes too. My friends and I all wanted to be heroes.

One example of this, portrayed in various forms, was a person who had been wounded in a battle. That person would say, "Leave me a canteen and a rifle and I will hold them off while you get away." "Go on, get out of here."

I didn't see this once or twice; I was surrounded by constant examples. These people believed that the good of the group was more important than what was good for them as individuals. Whether in real life, on television or in the movies, there were plenty of people who would volunteer to sacrifice themselves in one form or another so the good of the group would prevail. I wanted to grow up to be just like them. My friends did too.

I conducted a little experiment. I asked some people my age, "If I said to you, 'Leave me a canteen and a rifle.' what situation would I be in and what does it mean?"

Each of them answered that I would be in a group experiencing a conflict or battle of some kind. They concluded that I would be sacrificing myself so the others in the group might have a chance of escaping from the threat.

I asked some young people the same question. No one knew what I meant. One student replied, "Ummmm, you are thirsty and you want to shoot somebody?" The others didn't have an answer.

I suppose this doesn't really prove anything, at least not scientifically. I did find it a little disappointing however.

Perhaps I am wrong, but I don't see as many examples of heroes as I used to. There are acts of heroism being performed everyday, but they are usually ignored unless they are considered "exceptional".

We all experienced a period of hero appreciation after September 11th. I found that refreshing. Seeing people applauding while police and firemen passed was uplifting. Recently the death of former NFL player and soldier Pat Tillman reminded us what a hero looks like. He also reminded us that today heroes are often ignored until someone transcends "normal" heroism and gets our attention.

There was a time when heroism was actually considered "normal" and yet still revered. Do we not see much more selfishness today? There are more people than ever who couldn't care less about someone else's heroism. These are the folks who have no concept of "the good of the group."

The only thing they are interested in is getting what's theirs. Whether it be by acting rude, filing ridiculous lawsuits (attorneys standing by), whining, and such, these people are dedicated to only one thing—themselves. Their battle cry is "It's all about me!"

Am I the only American who feels saddened and discouraged by the prevalence of such behavior?

Would you take the canteen and a rifle?

Mating/Nesting

I am often struck by how funny humans are. For all of our pontificating, grandiose behaviors and proclamations of our superiority over all living creatures, we act just like them.

It strikes me often that if you strip away all the "flash" and "sizzle" from human beings what is left are many of the same behaviors seen each day in the animal kingdom.

As males we pump up our bodies, suck in our stomachs, primp and groom ourselves to gain the attention of as many females as we can. We parade in front of the female trying to impress her with our strength and good looks. (Good looking guys bug the rest of us!) Some might add wit, money, fame or power, but it's all for the same reason—to mate.

There you have it. Not much different than most other species is it? Sure there are men who want to have a home, have a relationship, perhaps even nurture their offspring. However, the bottom line is that most males are primarily looking for mating opportunities.

One reason for this is because that is how we are programmed. Another is for the sheer excitement of the hunt. Still another reason is conquest and ego building. The more women with whom a man mates, the more his seed is spread, and of course, the more he can brag about it. In nature that is what it is all about.

The only difference between male human beings and other male animals is that we also have a moral code and/or a spiritual side. This aspect of our existence can potentially lift the basic act of mating into the higher level of love and commitment. Usually there is a power struggle between the two. Most men have to learn or develop the skills of relationship building. The mating "skills" were already pro-grammed.

In an effort to gain the male's attention look what females are will-ing to do. They routinely apply varying colors to their faces to enhance their features. They color, straighten, curl, comb, brush, and primp their hair. They wear clothing, some of which is binding or uncomfort-able, to make their form more appealing to the male. Surgery and other medical procedures, dieting, and the like are part of many women's attempts to stay "matable".

However, whereas the males are looking for conquest and mating, most females are looking to nest. Generally speaking, women covet a home, a man, and children much more than a male would. Women want to be appealing to males. They want to find one, mate and then nest.

Of course I am simplifying much about men and women. As always, there are exceptions and even some changes taking place to this basic premise. However, right or wrong, good or bad this has been the basic foundation of human existence since the beginning of time.

The most obvious display of the "mating ritual" has never been more apparent than today at any dance club or school dance. If you have not been to either in recent years, my guess is that you would probably be shocked.

The accepted form of dancing today would have been considered obscene perhaps 30 years ago. Dancing today involves opposite sex or same sex couples basically rubbing their body parts against those of their partner's. One partner is usually facing away from the person with whom they are dancing so the buttocks of the first partner can be rubbed and pushed against the genital region of the second partner. This will sometimes include 3 or more dancers. The one in the middle will be receiving "attention" from the others who are encircling him/her. Put on some fur or feathers and you would think you were watch-ing *Animal Planet*.

Dancing today is nothing more than a manifestation of the mating ritual. The current trends have me wondering if the once innocent act of dancing has now become a symbol of the ever growing erosion of our society. Regardless, I can't see how this is a good thing.

Today's dancing is yet another breakdown of the barriers which once had to be overcome before "mating". It kind of reverses the whole "one step at a time" approach to sex. With most of the sexual contact between dancing partners already taking place, albeit in clothing, the only step left is kissing. When that step is added, it is no longer the first sexual act between two people, it now can be the last. The dancers had already been mimicking sexual acts throughout the evening.

Since this form of dancing is currently in vogue, participants in their early teens and older, whether they are casual friends or even strangers, will immediately engage in this behavior as soon as they hit the dance floor.

I think this is harmful because it breaks down the respect of the male and female for each other. It also weakens the fragile inhibitions that once had to be overcome before engaging in sexual activity.

This is just one of the reasons sex today is considered a "casual" activity. It's just like dancing only with less clothing. One other interesting aspect to high school dances is that the adult "chaperones" have long since given up on trying to curtail or contain this form of dancing. Perhaps they felt intimidated. Perhaps they didn't want to be like the adults in the past who claimed that "rock and roll" was indecent. In any event, since the students are permitted to dance in the way I just described, without objection from adults, there is an implied message to the students that their behavior is acceptable.

My we've come a long way from the days when a "gentleman" would put a handkerchief between his hand and the "lady's" waist.

Unfortunately, lack of mutual respect is not only evident in today's dancing. Males today are quite comfortable demeaning females; sometimes verbally, and other times physically.

Males will push or pull girls, even hit them whether playfully or out of anger. I have seen girls getting grabbed, groped, bumped into lockers, grabbed by their shoulders, pushed from behind, grabbed by the arm, swung around by their backpacks and the list goes on and on. Oftentimes the male is not intending any harm. It is just the way males are now treating females—at least at the middle and high school levels. Other times, they are intending harm with no regard to the fact that their actions are being directed towards a girl.

Whatever happened to "chivalry?" When I was growing up I was taught to always hold the door open for any female and any elder. When walking with a female, the male always positioned himself between the street and his female companion. A gentleman always helped a lady with her jacket or sweater. It was completely unacceptable to use profanity in the presence of a lady. Most importantly, it was never, ever acceptable to grab, push, strike, or bump a female. When did all of this change? Is it foolish of me to think chivalry was a good thing?

Males are not the only guilty ones however. I have also seen females become less concerned with their image and reputations. Girls today, by comparison to the recent past, have become more aggressive. They are becoming less mysterious, more forward and more willing to accept behaviors once frowned upon. Perhaps they view this new way of life as freedom.

They have become more flirtatious, expose more of their bodies and are much more willing to be sexually active. They are also more willing to be sexually adventurous. At many high school parties it is commonplace for two or more girls to engage in sexual activity just to put on a show. Triple kisses, and other forms of sexual activity are typical. The changes that have taken place in females are also evident at any "spring break" gathering.

If you have middle school or high school aged children they already know everything I just told you. If they say they didn't, they are lying.

Adults are partially to blame for these new behaviors. While the adults in the world were encouraging "safe" sex, the message our children were hearing was "casual" sex. The young people of today know they are supposed to use protection when they engage in intercourse. So, they have concluded if they do, then they are doing the right thing.

They have also come to the conclusion that any other form of sexual contact other than intercourse isn't actually "having sex". I think by now, thanks to programs like *Oprah*, we now know there is an epidemic in teens and preteens engaging in oral sex and thinking nothing of it. (See Bill Clinton).

Here is a statement spoken by a 14 year old female which illustrates this perfectly. She was walking with friends on her way to class when I overheard her say, "I am still a virgin, but my mouth isn't". If you think she is the exception, you need to get out more. I hear similar comments nearly everyday.

Adolescents today will engage in all forms of sexual contact—with the exception of intercourse—and feel that they are doing nothing wrong. There has also been an increase is same sex activity. Many adolescents today consider themselves to be "bi". It began when girl on girl sex was elevated from low budget porn movies to accepted cable and theatrical movie releases. It wasn't long before girls were kissing and fondling each other on popular tv shows. Now the practice is commonplace and can be seen virtually anywhere.

Guys still haven't overcome their reluctance for same sex activity to the degree girls have—so far. For the most part however, most teens will tell you that sex is sex and it feels good no matter how you do it or with whom you do it. Perhaps males and females are beginning to mirror each other with respect to "mating" and disregarding the "nesting" part. What's next?

It's the Little Things

For some reason, perhaps because we are so overwhelmed by the amount of crime, confusion and mayhem we face in our everyday lives, we have resorted to measuring in degrees just how bad an inappropriate behavior is. Of course lawyers and courts lead the way. Consequently we focus on the result—not on the act itself. I believe this is the root of the continued proliferation of the very evils we are trying to eradicate.

We split hairs so much today that the actual illegal or inappropriate action itself is being all but forgotten. I understand the intent, but I don't understand the logic.

If a person reaches into the belongings or the space of another person it shouldn't matter what was taken. Whether it was 10 cents or $1000 the act of invading another person's space or property is what is unacceptable. The penalty should be for the act, not for the net result.

Allow me to illustrate what I mean:

I only took $10.00. **(It's not the $10.00. It's that you put your hand in someone else's pocket).**

I only hit him once. **(It's not the "once". It's that you took your closed fist and smashed it into someone else's face.)**

It's just a small knife. **(It's not that size of the blade. It's that you used it to cut into another person's flesh)**

It wasn't even loaded. **(It's not that it wasn't loaded. It's that you pointed your gun at another person.)**

It was just a pair of earrings. They will never even miss them. **(It's not the earrings. It's that you consider them yours.)**

It was my first offense. (that you got caught). **(It's not that it's only your first time. It's that you chose to do it at all).**

I was only 10 minutes late. **(It's not about the 10 minutes. It's that you weren't early).**

We were using protection. (Minors) **(It's not that you were protecting yourself from diseases and unwanted pregnancy. It's that you didn't respect each other enough to wait.)**

I only plagiarized one page. **(It's not the one page. It's that you took someone else's work and put your name on it.)**

It's only 9 mph over the speed limit. It's not really speeding unless you are going 10 mph over the speed limit. **(If 9 mph over the speed limit isn't speeding, why did you suddenly slow down when you saw the police car in the median?)**

Everyone does it. **(It's not about everyone else doing it. It's about you doing it.)**

You can't prove it. **(It's not about me proving it. It's about you admitting it.)**

I don't know how most people would feel about this, but it seems to me that we could sure benefit by attaching consequences to the deed and not the result. Breaking a rule or a law is just that.

We have become a society of negotiators, bargainers, compromisers and avoiders. Consequently, very few people will admit to any wrongdoing or accept responsibility for their behavior. Even fewer will accept the consequence of their wrongdoing without comparing their punishment to that which others may have received. "Why did I get a ticket?" "My friend was stopped for speeding last month and he didn't get one."

This kind of thinking has to stop. Wrong is wrong. Bad is bad. Why do we ignore that? We need fewer formulas, increments, bargains, compromises, deals, distortions, and technicalities. We need to teach that every behavior has a consequence instead of every behavior has a list of potential consequences which may or may not be enforced or agreed to pending a review or appeal.

Pet Peeves

On a somewhat lighter note, here are some of my "pet peeves." I have so many that I actually considered writing an entire book about them. I narrowed the list down to the ones I hope you have too.

Perhaps when you read these you will feel comforted knowing that somewhere out there is another person who is thinking the same thoughts as you. Maybe that will ease your pain the next time you encounter one of them.

Political Commercials: I don't know about you, but I dread every election. Watching the candidates is painful enough. Watching their political commercials is almost unbearable. We are always being told that voter turnout is low at most elections. I wonder if it has anything to do with the effect political commercials has on us.

During an election year we are continuously battered by the incessant, self-serving, ridiculously over-played, and totally demeaning political commercials. By the time the election actually rolls around I no longer care which candidate wins. I am just happy the election is over!

I think we should pass a law that political advertising cannot begin until three months before an election. (I'm Jim Steger and I approve this paragraph because I believe by working together we can make politics better for all Americans.)

Disclaimers: This has driven me crazy for years, yet I have never heard anyone else ever mention it. It's those disclaimers on television commercials that are written so small that you can't read them. You can almost always find them in car commercials, but they are by no means the only ones. It's the text on the bottom of the screen that you will never be able to read in the time it is on the screen. Apparently there is some requirement that necessitates having the disclaimer there. However, there must be some kind of a loophole which permits the disclaimer to be printed too small to read. I want every company whose commercials contain such disclaimers to know that I pay no attention to anything you are selling in your ad. I make it a point to read as much of the disclaimer as I can in the time it is on the screen. Perhaps if more people did that, advertisers would finally enlarge the type so we could all more easily read it—thus enabling us to watch the rest of the commercial.

Speaking of disclaimers, what about the spoken disclaimers at the end of all of the drug commercials today? The frequency at which these commercials are being shown has skyrocketed. The disclaimers are either hideous or hilarious. I haven't decided which. When the side effects of a drug may cause, stomach pain, sexual side effects, nausea headache, fatigue, dry mouth, vomiting, skin rash—and the list goes on—I think I would rather deal with the ailment.

Rude People: Courtesy is not a weakness. Rudeness is not a strength. We have all seen people who seem to think that it is their right, or a way of expressing their independence and/or strength, by being rude. In its simplest form being rude is nothing more than immaturity mixed with selfishness. "I am in a hurry, get out of my way". "I want to see better so I will stand in front of you"

Have we all not heard of parking lot confrontations? Have you ever waited for a car to back out of a parking space at the mall or elsewhere only to have another car swoop in and take it right in front of you? To any person who is guilty of these or any other rude behaviors, you need to understand that you are selfish, immature, and unimportant. Get what you want, anyway you have to, but realize the rest of us disdain you. You are pollution. You are contaminating our society. We should all be given bright yellow stickers with the words, "STUPID/RUDE" on them. Every time we have to put up with you we should just slap one of these stickers on your back. That way we can warn other people who may encounter you.

Stupid People and Examples Thereof: Notice I didn't say "ignorant people". Ignorance is the result of not being taught. Stupidity is the result of refusing to learn. Ignorance is the absence of information. Stupidity is ignoring information. Ignorance can be corrected. Stupidity is untouchable.

People today embrace their stupidity. Stupid people and their lawyers are the folks who are responsible for all of the disclaimers we have to live with today. Because of these people we are told not to operate our motor vehicles with the windshield sunshades open. We are warned not to use our blow-dryers while taking a shower. We are told that the coffee we just ordered is "hot".

By the way, if you are wondering if I am worried that I might offend someone by these examples, the answer is, "No." Stupid people never think they are stupid. They will think I am stupid for mentioning these. Ah, the irony of it all.

Here are some examples of stupidity you certainly have encountered too!

Smokers: There is no way around this, smoking anything is stupid. There I said it. Maybe this habit could have been defended a number of years ago before all the scientific data we now have became available. Not anymore.

Smoking is the number one cause of preventable death in this country. If that weren't reason enough for an intelligent person not to smoke, smoking also makes the smoker, the smoker's clothes, and the smoker's house and car all smell bad.

Think about it, not only does smoking kill us, make us sick, and cause the offender to smell awful, but smokers are the only living creatures on the face of the planet stupid enough to voluntarily suck the smoke from a burning plant into their lungs. If you don't think that is stupid, remember this. Smokers not only suck the deadly gases and chemicals into their lungs, they actually pay a lot of money to do it! A smoker who smokes a pack a day, in twenty years will have spent no less than $146,000. Imagine setting fire to $146,000.

I have a suggestion. For $46,000 I will come over and hook you up to the tailpipe of your car. That way you save $100,000 and will still be able to enjoy smooth tobacco pleasure by breathing in many of the same chemicals found in cigarettes every time you start your car.

I wonder what would happen if each time someone lit up a cigarette everyone else around him/her burst into raucous laughter while pointing at the offender. Imagine seeing people on the street, on the subway, at the office, in a nightclub all pointing and laughing hysterically at someone foolish enough to light up a cigarette.

I don't understand why so many smokers pay no attention to the fact that their smoke is polluting the air, both in smell and visibility, of those around them.

In closing I would like every smoker to consider this. Whenever you are smoking in the proximity of others you are having the same effect on them as someone letting out a long, uninterrupted, smelly, cloudy fart. In your case, the rest of us don't need to sticker you. The odor that surrounds you already told us you were "Stupid/Rude".

Machine Talkers: It's one thing to talk to a car that is about to run out of gas, "Come on, baby. Just get me home and I will never let your tank get this low again." Okay, maybe that is a little crazy, but it's not necessarily stupid. Stupid is when a person talks to an ATM machine or automated answering machine thinking they will actually get an answer.

For example, the text on the ATM screen reads, "Please enter your PIN" which you did but forgot to hit "Enter". You reply (aloud), "I just did!"

You enter it again only this time you make a big production out of it by pressing each number harder and more dramatically, but again neglect to hit "Enter".

"Please enter your PIN"

"I just did you stupid machine!" Uh huh, the machine is stupid. Time to get stickered.

Grocery Blockers: I am a guy who actually enjoys grocery shopping. I particularly enjoy the vegetable sections. It's unfortunate that grocery stores are a haven for stupid people.

It amazes me that there are so many people who block the aisles in grocery stores with their carts and their bodies. They stop right next to a display case placed in the aisle. Consequently the person, their cart and the display case form an effective roadblock. Some realize their mistake and quickly move their cart, with or without an apology. The really stupid ones continue looking at the food items while you and the other shoppers all stand politely waiting for this imbecile to wake up.

Once one of these people exceeds 3 stickers they should be required to do their shopping between the hours of midnight and 5:00 am. Do you think 3 stickers is too lenient?

Air Travel Complicators: I often ask myself, "How did so many stupid people get the money to fly?" Airports and airlines have to be the mecca, the holy land, of stupidity and rudeness. When you are planning to travel by air, don't forget to bring a bunch of "Stupid/Rude" stickers.

When standing in the long winding lines waiting to get our bags checked, most of us relish finally getting to the front of the line. When we do, we scan the entire length of the counter in front of us, like starving animals of prey, looking for the next available agent.

Many of us even take a step or two in the direction of the attendant who just finished handing the ticket envelope to the person he/she was assisting. Once we see the hand go up, we burst into a full speed walk.

Why are there so many people who once they finally get to the front of the line are unaware that one of the attendants who is available is waving frantically trying to get their attention? People, it's not that difficult!

Don't stand there reading your book, or talking away with people you know—or worse—with people you don't know (like me). Don't be shuffling through your purse or briefcase looking for your ID when you had plenty of time to do so earlier. Pay attention.

Being first in line carries a certain amount of responsibility. If you are unable to handle this, kindly step aside and ask the person behind you to let you know when it's your turn to go. Then be gracious enough to pause a moment so that person can apply the "Stupid/Rude" sticker you deserve.

<u>Walkway Blockers:</u> Why are there so many stupid people who stand in the way of you getting by on the movable walkways in airports? Doesn't everybody know that you stand <u>to the right</u> if you are going to stand and not walk? By moving yourself to the right, it allows people who want to walk on the movable walkway to pass you by and continue on. Why is this so difficult? And finally, if you are one of the people who enjoys walking on these walkways, please don't trip or stumble when you reach the end. Okay, the first time may be acceptable, but not after that.

If you insist on clogging up the movable walkways, kindly stand for a moment with your back to the walkway once you reach the end so the rest of us can slap a "Stupid/Rude" sticker on you as we pass by.

<u>Lavatory Loungers:</u> How many more times will I have to endure seeing people form a line at the forward lavatory only seconds after the flight attendant finished asking everyone not to?

"Please do not form a line at the forward lavatory. FAA safety regulations prohibit people from standing at the front of the aircraft. Please wait until the forward lavatory is unoccupied before coming forward to use it."

It never fails. The pilot turns off the "seatbelt" light and invariably one person gets up and walks into the forward lavatory. That's when I clench my jaw and hold my breath. Sure enough, another person gets up and walks up to the lavatory and stands outside the closed door.

Who are these people? Do they think the rules only apply to the rest of us? Are they that defiant or is it possible they are that stupid?

The rest of us should be allowed to slap a "Stupid/Rude" sticker on their backs as they walk all the way down the aisle back to their seats.

Overhead Compartment Crammers: This one the airlines are actually cracking down on. Only stupid or rude people insist on jamming their oversized "carry on" bags into the overhead compartment. This goes way beyond getting stickered. Come to think of it, perhaps flight attendants should be issued the same kind of tasers used by police officers. After all they put up with almost as much inappropriate behavior as many police officers.

Every person trying to jam an oversized bag into the overhead compartment, holding up the line, and taking up all the space in the compartment should be zapped by the flight attendant. I bet the problem would be solved in a matter of weeks. Okay, that may be a little optimistic.

Stupid People Who Sue For Stupid Reasons: I am thinking about suing all the stupid people who have caused the rest of us so much stress, anguish and frustration after hearing about the stupid lawsuits they filed.

As we all know, there was a lawsuit against McDonalds filed by a lady because she was "burned" by the hot coffee in the cup she put between her legs while in the car.

Other people have sued fast food restaurants claiming that is the restaurants' fault for making them fat. A woman is suing a casino because she claims that it's the casino's fault she is losing so much money while gambling. A man who murdered his family, and then beheaded each of them is suing the police for being "too rough" with him during the arrest.

Such ridiculous lawsuits are bad enough. There is something even worse however. The people on the juries who actually find in favor of the poor "victims". Knock it off already. Doesn't everyone understand that regardless whether a jury "sticks it" to a big corporation or to a small company we are the ones who end up paying?

Motor Vehicle Departments: Customer service can still be found in many businesses today. It's refreshing when we are treated like we are appreciated.

For some reason, customer service is not a priority at most motor vehicle departments. What each of us has to endure while waiting in one of their lines makes a doctor's office seem like Disneyland!

Is there anything that weighs more heavily on us than knowing that our driver's license is about to expire? I do have an idea though.

I think a corporation like McDonalds should be given the contract to handle driver's licenses and registrations.

Have you ever been waiting in line at McDonalds and just when you got to the front and were ready to order the person taking orders went on "their break."? Have you ever waited in line while a McDonalds' employee sat off to the side and drank a cup of coffee while reading the paper?

Motor Vehicle Departments could learn from fastfood restaurants, but they never will. They don't have to.

Fake churchgoers: It has always bewildered me how so many people self-select the information they want to hear regarding faith or religion and discard the rest. I think they are commonly referred to as "hypocrites". They have been around since the beginning of religion itself.

These are the people who seem to think their bad behavior is different than the bad behavior of everyone else in the world. They believe that they only act inappropriately because they were forced to by the actions of lesser people. They think that God Himself understands and supports their behaviors.

Here is one, small example that I have noticed since I was child. How can a person leave a place of worship, get into his/her car and then be so concerned about getting out of the parking lot that they either squeeze in front of someone or pass by other vehicles that are trying to get into the same line?

I can understand how this kind of situation might happen at the mall or at a sporting event. In a church parking lot? Wouldn't you think that a church parking lot would be the last place you would ever experience someone acting rude or inconsiderate?

Reality TV: What a misleading title that is! Am I the only person who knows there is nothing real about "reality" tv? Am I expected to believe, that in spite of cameras, sound equipment, and in many cases, the presence of crew members, the people I am watching are all acting completely honestly and naturally?

Please stop using the term "reality" tv to refer to such shows. Reality TV is when a politician says what he really thinks or tells an "off color" joke while unaware that the microphones were still on. Reality TV is what we see when watching video from surveillance cameras.

If we must have reality shows, let's at least have one that will do some good. I suggest that we do a reality show in a prison. Let's all watch, via hidden cameras, what really goes on each day and night behind the walls and in the cells twenty-four hours a day in a real prison with real prisoners and guards. That would be *Reality TV.*

Such a program should be mandatory viewing for all school aged children. It might prevent some of them from ending up there.

From Winners to Whiners

Too many Americans whine about not having enough stuff. They whine about not getting any breaks. They whine about having jobs they don't enjoy. Most whiners are people who are taking everything they do have for granted.

Americans have access to every necessity and to almost every luxury life has to offer. What's worse, in my opinion, is that too many Americans ignore the opportunities available to each of us in this country.

It is not at all uncommon to hear people who were born in this country claim they didn't get a fair shake. Yet on the other hand, people from other countries continue to immigrate to America and proceed to quickly establish themselves and their families in some kind of a successful business.

Many of these immigrants have limited skills in the English language. They are unfamiliar with our customs and laws. They are unfamiliar with real estate deals, closings, insurance, taxes, licensing and other aspects of business.

They have to hope and trust that the people with whom they are dealing treat them fairly. They have to overcome getting cheated on a regular basis until they catch on.

In spite of all these disadvantages, many immigrants lead wonderfully successful lives filled with appreciation for this "land of opportunity."

Two of the best examples of the potential for success available to everyone in America are Arnold Swartzenegger and Oprah Winfrey.

We all know that Mr. Swartzenegger immigrated to this country and through hard work and determination overcame each disadvantage and setback he faced. He became extraordinarily successful in two of our most challenging fields, show business and politics.

He is not only a multimillionaire; he is also governor of California. Many of us had a "head start" but he passed us all by.

Even though Ms Winfrey was born in America she was raised surrounded by poverty. She overcame three major disadvantages as she was working her way up the entertainment/corporate ladder. She was poor, she is black and she is a woman.

Imagine the number of obstacles Ms. Winfrey had to overcome that many of us have never had to face at all. Yet she has become one of the most successful individuals in America.

Millions of women—and men—of all races consider her to be one of our greatest role models. She is admired by millions. Ms. Winfrey is a daily reminder to all of us what can be achieved by anyone in this country if they are determined to be winners.

Think of that the next time you are tempted to whine about something.

It's all about Perspective

Here is a valuable lesson I learned later in life. We all have days when we feel like life has passed us by. We are frustrated in our jobs. We don't have enough money. Things always seem to be breaking down. Costs are always going up. Traffic is irritating. No one appreciates us. The kids take us for granted.

Even worse, it seems that people who are less moral, less intelligent and less hardworking always seem to have more than the rest of us. I used to feel that way quite often—until I realized that it's all about perspective.

Two well-publicized tragedies not only changed the lives of those involved, they also changed my life as well. These events were the accident which occurred to the actor Christopher Reeve in May of 1995 and the death of Princess Diana in a car crash in August 1997.

You may recall that Mr. Reeve fell from a horse resulting in his paralysis. He has been confined to a wheel chair ever since. Some years later Mr. Reeve wrote a book entitled, "Still Me". Christopher Reeve is a man who is much wealthier than I. He's better looking, more traveled, and more influential. He was living the "American Dream". He had the kind of life I wanted.

You probably think the lesson I learned from him was that I am better off than a man who became paralyzed. Not quite. The lesson I learned from Mr. Reeve was much more powerful than just being grateful that I had my health.

In his book, Mr. Reeve mentioned that one of his most coveted goals, a goal that motivates him everyday to fight through his humiliation and block out feelings of anger and self-pity, is to one day be able to hug his son. This handsome, successful, wealthy, influential, movie star has been hoping and struggling each day for years to do something I can do at any time, everyday with no effort at all.

After the death of Princess Diana I was struck by how devastating her death was to Prince William and Prince Harry. The world may have lost a princess-celebrity, but the two princes lost their cherished mother. All of their power and wealth would not, could not change that.

I imagined that if Prince William had been given the chance to have his mother returned to him by trading places with me he would have jumped at the chance. He would gladly relinquish the castles, the wealth, the freedom, the power, and virtually everything else that seemed so important to me. Prince William would have traded everything he had in exchange for the life I have. That opened my eyes.

Who would have thought that I am better off than a dashing movie star and the future King of England?

We are So Jaded

I am very bothered by the way so many of us take for granted great achievements. I am not talking about the glamorous achievements of athletes or movie stars. I am referring to those not so glamorous, yet life-changing achievements we seem to ignore.

Achievements in medicine, science, architecture, mathematics, and other such accomplishments just don't seem to excite, motivate or inspire us. Here is one example:

Recently, the U.S. successfully landed a space probe on the planet Mars. Did you hear that? The United States successfully shot a rocket-propelled probe into outer space. It successfully landed on a moving planet some 35 million miles away. That alone is astounding. It gets even better.

After landing, this machine righted itself and began taking pictures! It was then able to send those pictures all the way back to Earth. It also responded to instructions and communications sent by people back on earth. Our scientists were actually "talking to it!" Later it began to move about and take soil samples!

Sure it made the news, but where was all the hoopla? Where was the fanfare? Why did something that astonishing, that marvelous, receive so much less attention than a "pop star's" trial or another's "quickie" marriage?

Where were the tickertape parades? Why didn't the people involved in this monumental achievement become instant celebrities? Why was this history-making feat overshadowed by a "wardrobe malfunction"?

Have our priorities really slipped so low? Have we become so jaded by special effects that we are no longer awed by reality? Apparently the fact that this landing was real doesn't mean that much to many of us.

I was thinking of times in the past when everyone gathered around their radios or televisions and had goose bumps as they listened to or watched some extraordinary moment in time. Moments like those brought us together. It uplifted our spirits. It inspired us.

Such examples include Lindbergh crossing the Atlantic, Neil Armstrong and Buzz Aldrin walking on the moon, the successful return of Apollo 13, and the first return and landing of the space shuttle. We don't respond much to such achievements any longer. I guess we have "seen" it all before in movies, on television and in video games.

It's too bad we don't distinguish between reality and make-believe.

Thoughts to Think about

I thought I would share some of my homespun "words of wisdom" with you. These are thoughts, sayings and ideas that make sense to me. I hope they will to you as well.

If you are not in a hospital—or worse—in the waiting room of a hospital, the rest is gravy.

What doesn't kill you usually hurts.

Kids are like grass. If you don't watch them they will end up in all the places you don't want them.

If you're going to cook some bacon, you're going to get some grease on the stove.

You will never get caught if you aren't doing it. You will never be caught with something you don't have. You will never be caught in a place you aren't at.

The internet brings strangers together but separates families. Think about that.

I have a theory based on the Roadrunner and Coyote cartoons. If you ever saw them you will remember that the coyote would come up with perfectly good plans to catch the roadrunner. Invariably each would fail for one reason or another. It would drive me crazy that after failing, the coyote would never try the same plan again.

The rocket skates were a perfectly good idea. He just needed to stay away from trucks and boulders. With a few adjustments the magnetic bird seed would have worked like a charm. (Avoiding cliff edges would have also helped).

The point is—don't be like the coyote. When you want something keep trying until you get that damn roadrunner!

I had a student ask me a very interesting question one day after reciting the "Pledge of Allegiance". He turned to me and said, "Once you have pledged allegiance to something, should you ever have to say it again? I thought that was a very profound question.

I understand why schools often include the reciting of the pledge in their daily announcements. However, in its purest form, pledging one's allegiance should mean just that. In principle it shouldn't be necessary or even expected to do so everyday.

Also, reciting the pledge has become a meaningless ritual in most schools. It's just another opportunity for those who want to be "individuals" to express themselves.

Since we are so worried about being politically correct today, students are allowed to ignore the pledge. They can sit, turn away or even stand with faces filled with boredom. We allow it. We don't want to risk any lawsuits. Do you think saying the pledge everyday fosters patriotism or could doing so actually demean it? In any event, I like that student's take—allegiance once pledged is forever.

I have one more thing I want to say regarding "The Pledge".

Whenever I see someone who was born in America ignore the "Pledge of Allegiance" or the playing of the "National Anthem" as some kind of expression of their political or moral principles I am offended.

This is nothing more than a cheap little demonstration of a pompous, disrespectful person slapping the face of the country in which they willingly accept every freedom and luxury presented to them.

To each of you I say, "Choose some other, more meaningful way to show us how moral and righteous you are. Being rude is so tiring."

To anyone who came to this country and then chooses to ignore our rituals and traditions, please, all I ask is a little respect and consideration.

If I were to ever find myself in a country to which I freely journeyed I would happily stand for their national anthem, or take part in whatever other rituals or customs that were important to them. Doing so wouldn't make me any less American.

Being respectful doesn't mean you are less of a person anymore than being disrespectful indicates you are a person of principle.

We would all be much better off if there were more courtesy and consideration and less disrespect and grandiose displays of individual arrogance.

Here is an interesting little tale. The next time you think the only luck you have is bad luck or the only timing you have is bad timing, just remember Philip Saville and Henry Ian Cusick. In case you are in the rather large group of people who do not who these gentlemen are read on.

Both are extraordinarily accomplished in their respective crafts. They worked together pouring their hearts into a monumentally expensive and breath-taking project. No detail was ignored. Shortcuts were not even considered.

Their labor, coupled with the skills of many other gifted artists, produced a masterpiece. I am sure everyone involved in this exceptional project had fantasies about the worldwide acclaim they would receive as their work was discovered. It didn't happen.

You see, Philip Seville directed a potential blockbuster of a movie and Henry Ian Cusick was chosen to be its star. It was the role of a lifetime. This inspired production was the story of Jesus Christ's life—and death on the cross.

The movie was called, *The Gospel of John*. Have you heard of it? It was released at virtually the same time as another movie you may have heard of, *The Passion of the Christ*.

As we all know, Mel Gibson's "Passion" is expected to top 400 million dollars in the U.S. alone. On the other hand, "Gospel" has so far taken in just over 5 million dollars.

I can't help but wonder how Mr. Saville and Mr. Cusick were feeling when everywhere they turned they were faced with "Passion's" promos, posters, publicity and profits. It must have felt like walking away from a slot machine after playing it for hours only to have the next person hit the million dollar jackpot. I wonder what their next project will be.

Double Standard Death Sentences

I have been perplexed by the conflicting "message" implied by a mounting wave of public sentiment to do away with the death penalty, and the ongoing insistence that abortion is every woman's "right." I have tried, but I just cannot see how a reasonable society can justify both positions.

Not only is abortion accepted, there are multitudes of impassioned people proclaiming that each woman has the "right to choose" abortion because "…it's my body." To me this is a manifestation of the same "it's all about me" mentality that is so prevalent today.

Too many people concerned only with their individual "needs" will ignore the well-being of others in a family, a workplace, a team, a school, a community, and a country. To them the only thing that matters is getting "what they are entitled to."

The same "logic" is evident when a person chooses abortion because a pregnancy presents an "inconvenience." Abortion is an easy way out—at least for the woman.

By the way I don't accept the attitude that a man's opinion on abortion doesn't matter because it is a women only issue. What a horrific display of close-minded selfishness. The last time I checked, in addition to the woman involved, every pregnancy (with a few exceptions) included a man and at least one fetus. It is far from being as simple as some people would like us to believe.

No matter what your view may be on when "life" begins, there is no doubt that something or someone is being "terminated", destroyed and disposed of in every abortion. Yet it is occurring everyday while its supporters march in the streets clamoring for this practice to be protected from any interference.

All the while many of the same people will picket, protest, and pontificate that the death penalty is "cruel and unusual punishment." People proclaim that we are a civilized society and that putting a criminal to death is barbaric. We protect a fully developed life of evil while abandoning a yet to fully develop life dependent on someone else's love for its very survival. Perhaps we are more barbaric than we would like to admit.

As a society we seem more determined to protect murderers, spotted owls, silvery minnows and endangered plants than we are unborn humans. I just don't get it. Perhaps it's just easier to "protect" grown men and women who destroyed other lives than it is to protect still-developing humans who never lived life at all.

Could it be said that in our "civilized" society it is actually safer being a murderer than it is being unborn?

(If you like statistics here is one for you. In the year 2003, there were 65 convicts put to death in the United States. During that same year there were an estimated 1,300,000 abortions.)

Death-Lying Naked on a Table

Everyone is going to die. We all understand that. We don't often think about it, but we do realize it. Each one of us will have our turn. It is inescapable. Like it or not, each and every one of us is standing in a line that will lead us to the moment when we too will be lying naked on a table.

There are people in front of us and people behind us. Each day, each hour, each minute we are moving our way in that line edging ever closer to our final moment. The trick to this line is that we don't know where, when or how it ends.

From superstar to servant, from business mogul to delivery boy, from saint to sinner—we all end up on that table. No one escapes. Sounds pretty dire doesn't it?

It all depends how you look at it. For those of us who believe this life is only a temporary stay in our ultimately eternal journey, death isn't so intimidating. Others who believe that this life is all there is can still find much to be excited about.

Either way I don't think there are too many of us who relish the idea of dying. However, part of me is somewhat intrigued by the possibilities. What if the Bible turns out to be right?

What if there is a heaven—and they let me in? What an exciting thing that would be! I must admit I am "dying" to find out the ultimate truth. Whenever I hear of someone's death I invariably think, "Now they know."

If it's true that we will end up with our loved ones, surrounded by all the other souls in heaven that will be pretty great. I am not embarrassed to say that I would love to meet God and thank Him for everything! I would certainly look up family members and other loved ones.

Not long afterward I would go over and introduce myself to a host of people I always wanted to meet (assuming they made it).

Do you find it strange that there are more ways to die today than ever before? Have you ever wondered if yours will be a "normal" death? Has it occurred to anyone else that as we continue to "evolve" we are now dying primarily in ways that once did not exist?

In addition to "bizarre" deaths like getting sucked out of plane, or getting hit by a tire at an auto race, consider the leading causes of death in America and what this says about us. Americans are dying everyday from smoking, car accidents, obesity, suicides, homicides, drugs/alcohol, and diseases which for the most part are the results of our lifestyles.

Whatever happened to dying from "natural causes?" It seems virtually impossible for anyone to die of old age, peacefully in their sleep anymore.

Will you die an untimely death at the hands of a careless or violent human? Will you pass away as the result of your lifestyle? Will your death be the result of a "freak" accident? Will it involve terror? Will you know you are dying or will it happen so fast that you didn't even realize you died?

Knowing that death is the only certainty in life should compel us to live our lives concentrating on joy, love, laughter and peace.

We should be quick to laugh, and slow to anger. We should be eager to forgive and reluctant to retaliate. We should seek harmony and turn away from selfishness. We should be willing to give, happy to share and be grateful for the opportunities to do both. We should embrace challenge and fear no failure. We should be intrigued by adventure and avoid recklessness. We should stand for something, yet be willing to kneel to something greater.

Instead we spend much of our time and effort in pursuit of things which we forget are temporary, shallow, and meaningless. As much as we all aspire to be rich—and I include myself in that group—wealth and the accumulation of material things always ends the same way. There is an anecdote which summarizes this reality very nicely.

It seems that after the death of a well known, powerful, wealthy man, his accountant was asked, "How much did he leave?" The accountant replied, "All of it."

Don't get me wrong. I fully realize being wealthy is better than being poor. I am just saying be careful what you trade in your pursuit of wealth. There are many things in life that once traded cannot be returned. If you can die happy and rich—go for it. If not, go for happy.

Life is full of fantastic opportunities. Each day unfolds like a flower revealing truths, knowledge, love, adventure and wonder. There are also challenges, fears and failures. But when you look at these realistically you can see that the setbacks and disappointments are the very reasons accomplishments and successes feel so good. There is a beautiful balance in all of life.

Every life begins full of meaning, but too many lives end empty of meaning. Each of us started out innocently. Look at how many of us grew to embrace corruption. We began pure and end up contaminated.

The beauty of life, however, is that each day is a chance to begin anew. Don't let your chances pass you by unused and unfulfilled. Too many of us are letting too many of our days slip away unlived and unappreciated. What a waste.

This much is certain. You and I are going to die. Live your life so you will be missed. Live so your life mattered. It's not about how much you were able to get. It's about how much you were able to give.

Conclusion

If we accept that our parents and/or our grandparents were part of "The Greatest Generation" written about by Mr. Tom Brokaw, then I don't understand why we have abandoned virtually every principle, practice and philosophy in parenting, education, and law that helped to mold and shape them.

If it is a fair assumption that we did indeed abandon many of the practices that once produced such a successful generation, is it too late to go back to some or all of them?

Isn't it true that we have had more experts in their respective fields in the past twenty years than at any other time in history? Has all the advice and information they have been giving us regarding education, parenting and law been helping us?

Are the experts responsible for any of the trends we see today? People sometimes tend to believe that the "newest" idea is the most correct. Maybe we are finding out that isn't always the case.

Let's review. America has a drug problem. America has a crime problem. America has problems in the family, in education, in our courts and in our government. There are scandals in our corporations, in our military and in our religious institutions. There is a major chasm between adults and children.

Many Americans are tired, frustrated and discouraged. Is America on its last legs? How do you think things are going?

These concerns compelled me to write this book. I couldn't just sit back and watch as our country slowly disappeared into the shadows of mediocrity.

This isn't about blame. It doesn't matter to me how we got here. The fact is we're here. Now is the time for us to become less afraid to speak the truth, and become more willing to hear the truth.

I certainly do not have all the answers and there are many things I could still learn and improve upon. All I can say is that I am trying. I am open. I am optimistic. But there are too many threats hovering over us to ignore. I don't think we can just keep hoping that someone else will take care of our problems.

At the very least, by writing this book I have tried to alter some of the perceptions and some of the attitudes that may be responsible for the way things are.

I hope you will think of what I wrote the next time a criminal is set free or given a meaningless sentence. I want you to feel as I do when you see someone whining.

Do you feel differently about drugs and alcohol now? What about our policies in education? Are you ready to speak up against the trends in our society which are rampaging through the lives of our children?

We have reached a time when you must stand up for what you believe. You will have to choose to continue the way we have been going or step out of the line and start stumbling in a new direction. As for me, I would rather get lost trying to find some place better than stay on the path that has taken me here.

I'm just an average guy who took a chance. I shared my fears, my opinions and my thoughts; thoughts I hope you've had too, hoping to make a difference. Now all I can do is wait to see what happens next......

0-595-32102-X